Penguin Special
Star Wars

PROFESSOR DOROTHY HODGKIN, ~~...~~ ~~...~~ ~~...~~ ~~...~~ crystal-
lographer, Chancellor of Bristol Unive~~...~~ ~~...~~ ~~...~~ Nobel Laureate (1964). She
is President of the Pugwash Conferences on Science and World Affairs,
founded by Einstein and Russell, which bring together eminent scientists
from every part of the world to exchange views on nuclear weapons and
disarmament.

RIP BULKELEY is a research student working on the history of American
military space policy at King's College, London. He is a member of the
SANA Space Weapons Group and of the National Executive of CND.
Besides contributions to peace research journals, he has written *The Anti-
Ballistic Missile Treaty, 1972–1983* and *The Valley Path*.

JOHN PIKE is the Associate Director for Space Policy at the Federation of
American Scientists, and has been Convenor of its Space Policy Working
Group. A former political consultant and writer, he is the author of numerous
studies and articles on space and national security policy, and has recently co-
authored (with Thomas K. Longstreth and John B. Rhinelander) *The Impact
of U.S. and Soviet Ballistic Missile Defense Programs on the ABM Treaty*.

BEN THOMPSON is a musician and freelance computer programmer. During
1980–83 he was book-keeper for END, and was active in making links with
the Italian peace movement and campaigning against the cruise missile base at
Comiso, Sicily.

E. P. THOMPSON is a freelance writer and historian, a founder of END,
and a Vice-President of CND. He is a Foreign Honorary Member of the
American Academy of Arts and Sciences. He is the author of several books,
including *The Making of the English Working Class* and *Whigs and Hunters*
(both Penguin); he co-edited (with Dan Smith) the Penguin Special, *Protest
and Survive*, and among recent publications on peace questions are *The Heavy
Dancers* and *Double Exposure* (both Merlin Press).

STAR WARS

RIP BULKELEY
JOHN PIKE
BEN THOMPSON
E. P. THOMPSON (Editor)

WITH A FOREWORD BY
DOROTHY HODGKIN, OM

PENGUIN BOOKS

Penguin Books Ltd, Harmondsworth, Middlesex, England
Viking Penguin Inc., 40 West 23rd Street, New York, New York 10010, U.S.A.
Penguin Books Australia Ltd, Ringwood, Victoria, Australia
Penguin Books Canada Ltd, 2801 John Street, Markham, Ontario, Canada L3R 1B4
Penguin Books (N.Z.) Ltd, 182 190 Wairau Road, Auckland 10, New Zealand

First published 1985

Made and printed in Great Britain by
Richard Clay (The Chaucer Press) Ltd, Bungay, Suffolk
Typeset in Monophoto Ehrhardt

Contents

Dorothy Hodgkin   Foreword   7

1   E. P. Thompson   Why is Star Wars?   9

2   Ben Thompson   What is Star Wars?   28

3   John Pike   Assessing the Soviet ABM
    Programme   50

4   Rip Bulkeley   The Effects of SDI on
    Disarmament   68

5   E. P. Thompson   Folly's Comet   93

Abbreviations and Acronyms   146
Notes   147
Acknowledgements   159

Foreword

Dorothy Hodgkin, OM

On 6 August 1985 *Le Monde* devoted a whole page to the fortieth anniversary of the dropping of the first atomic bomb on Hiroshima: '*Il y a quarante ans, Hiroshima*'. On the page there were three articles, one on the strategic consequences of the bombing, one on the Manhattan project, the organization of 150,000 scientists, and the third on the present situation – the growth of the atomic arsenals, tens of thousands of bombs between the two great powers and some hundreds for Great Britain, France and China, the development of new varieties of bomb, large and small, and the enormous increase in the precision of delivery methods. Jacques Isnard ends with the words:

> In this arena, as in others, man's inventive spirit has been given free rein since 1945 and no international negotiation for disarmament has been able to hinder it. Space only, up to now, has escaped from the nuclear arms race, in not becoming a permanent depository for arms capable of producing massive destruction, suspended above humanity. Forty years after Hiroshima, earth and sea are full of them. For how long can space be spared?

A note of desperate pessimism runs through the article.

Only a few years ago we had thought space was safe, covered by the 1967 agreements between the great powers. We were quite hopeful, after the United Nations General Session for Disarmament in 1978, that real disarmament might soon begin. The events that changed this situation are described by Edward Thompson, extraordinary, fantastic as they are, in two historical chapters, the first giving the sequence of the events leading to President Reagan's speech on the Strategic Defence Initiative – 'Star Wars' – the latter concerned with the recent reactions of the nations, the present situation. The three central chapters cover first, by Ben Thompson, the scientific and technical features of the proposals to construct a defence in space against nuclear missiles, second, by John Pike, the present position of the Soviet programme in the field of defence against missiles and its relation to 'Star Wars', and third, by Rip Bulkeley, the different treaties already agreed by the great powers, and particularly the Anti-Ballistic Missile, ABM, Treaty of 1972, which are threatened by the Strategic Defence Initiative.

I cannot say that I agree with everything that is written in this book but I am in agreement with its purpose – to show the tremendous difficulties of setting up defence in space against nuclear weapons, the absurdity of even thinking of doing so for the alleged purpose of eventually ridding the world of nuclear weapons, much more easily done by direct methods. At the Los Alamos commemoration of the fortieth anniversary of the Manhattan Project H. Rabi said, 'History is a very important thing because by the perusal of history you can see the greatness and the folly of humanity.' If we see, as we should, from these pages, the folly of the Strategic Defence Initiative, we should surely act to keep space free of weapons and also to set free man's inventive spirit to work in other fields where problems, often most fascinating, remain to be solved for the good of mankind.

I might perhaps add a footnote to Edward Thompson's fears that the peace movement is slow to respond to present changes. There have already appeared, as he records, responses from among the scientists, who know best what difficulties and delusions are involved in SDI: Professor Bethe is one of many individuals who have written articles, and from West and East come almost daily new small pamphlets. And in July 1984 a meeting took place in Göttingen of leading scientists from many parts of the world. It issued an appeal to prevent all weapons in outer space and this has already been signed by 8,000 scientists in twenty-one countries. The covering letter from the Verantwortung für den Frieden Naturwissenschaftlicher Initiative ends with the words:

Now is the time to remember we are responsible not only for our own deeds, but also for those actions we accept without resistance. We are still in time to avoid the destabilizing development and a new type of arms race.

I hope this book helps.

September 1985

1 · Why is Star Wars?

E. P. Thompson

Star Wars or Strategic Defence Initiative (SDI) crept up on the world by stealth. Although the project was first announced by President Reagan in a speech to the American nation on 23 March 1983, little notice was then taken of it except in the United States.

At first sight, and at second sight, it looked as if it was the product of a satirist on human perversity rather than the vision of a statesman. For SDI envisages that in some twenty or thirty years, after expending some hundreds of billions of dollars, United States technology will emerge with an impermeable shield against incoming ballistic missiles.

It was admitted that the high-tech space-fic machinery for this was either at a primitive and untested stage or else was hypothetical. But these doubts were dashed aside by President Reagan's first and most influential convert, Caspar Weinberger, US Secretary of Defense, who – four days after the President's speech – affirmed his robust confidence that American technology could do whatever the President asked of it:

> There have been a lot of people who have derided our ability to reach the moon. But, fortunately, we had President Kennedy at that time, who took the position that this not only could but should be done. And a very few years later, we did it. So I don't have any real doubts of the American ability to do this.[1]

That did not altogether settle the matter, because, as irreverent American critics have pointed out, the moon was scarcely in a position to develop counter-measures to President Kennedy. The moon could not fight back. But 'the enemy' or 'the Russians' might find ways of destroying all this delicate space furniture, tricking the sensors and giving the radar migraines. And 'a platoon of hostile moon-men with axes' could have made the Apollo moon landing 'a disaster'.[2]

Moreover, the Russians might even perceive the objective of this protracted research and development to be threatening. For if America was really going to turn up one day with an impermeable shield, then (just like the moon) they would have no means of fighting back. In their eyes the United States would then be in a position to nuke the USSR with impunity.

That – Caspar Weinberger explained – was the typically jaundiced view to be expected of Commie propagandists. 'The reason the Soviets have no need to worry is that they know perfectly well that we will never launch a first strike.' All rational strategic thinking must commence from the first proposition that the Soviets are evil and are lusting to aggress, whereas the U S of A is inherently moral, for ever and ever, amen.

On the other hand, if the *Russians* were to develop an impermeable shield in advance of the Americans, then the most jaundiced view would be in order. Weinberger said (in December 1983) that 'unilateral' Soviet development of defences against ballistic missiles 'would be one of the most frightening prospects I could imagine'. And in January 1985 the White House issued a document which said that if the Soviet Union were to deploy a nationwide anti-ballistic defence, 'deterrence would collapse, and we would have no choices between surrender and suicide'.[3] Dr Edward Teller, who presided over the development of the first H-bomb, had already stated this succinctly in 1962 in his book, *The Legacy of Hiroshima*:

> If the Communists should become certain that their defences are reliable and at the same time know that ours are insufficient, Soviet conquest of the world would be inevitable.

These propositions (their nukes are bad nukes but ours are good) are, like those enshrined in the Declaration of Independence, 'self-evident'. Nevertheless, public relations required that some regard be paid to those who might be influenced by Commie propaganda. And at a press conference (29 March 1983) six days after unveiling Star Wars President Reagan suggested, in a rhetorical aside, that at the point when SDI became effective the USA might generously reveal the technology to the USSR so that it could have an impermeable shield too. However, it is not yet certain that Mr Reagan will still be President in the year 2010. He could, no doubt, circumvent the US Constitution but he may have more difficulty in circumventing his own.

It was generally assumed that Reagan's aside was jocular, and the defence experts threw themselves about. George W. Ball, a former US Under-Secretary of State, has suggested that the President put forward the idea at his press conference 'on the spur of the moment', and even White House advisers regarded it as 'the eccentric musing of a lovable leader, a benevolent quirk to be indulgently overlooked'.[4] And overlooked it has been, from that time to this. We hear no more about transferring technology to the USSR but a great deal about the dangers of transferring US technology to Western Europe (see p. 118). According to *The New York Times*, 'officials' say that Mr Reagan is 'no longer willing to share the technology with Moscow because it could be put to many other military and civilian uses' – or, in other words, the Pentagon has put the stopper on the White House.[5]

What the President did, more seriously, propose was that when the impermeable shield (or shields) were in place, *then*, at last, some measures of nuclear disarmament might commence. Since the nukes could no longer get through, and would be useless, there could be a build-down on both sides. So that it was solemnly proposed that, at astronomic cost, an astral venture should be set in motion to achieve an end – the blocking of each other's missiles – which could be achieved tomorrow, at no cost at all, by a rational agreement by both sides to disarm.

THE FIRST MILITARIZATION OF SPACE

It is clear that Star Wars, in this form, was the President's own brainchild. It did not arise from the Pentagon, nor even from the military–industrial complex (although strong interests had long been at work). At that moment, 23 March 1983, it came out of the top of President Reagan's head.

General Haig, who was Secretary of State at the time, has said that the speech was made with scarcely any preparation. 'I know the aftermath the next day in the Pentagon, where they were all rushing around saying, "What the hell is strategic defence?" '[6] Those in the Pentagon who did in fact know a great deal about elements of strategic defence – BMD (ballistic missile defence), ASAT (anti-satellite weapons) and other space operations – had not been consulted or informed. The Joint Chiefs of Staff had made no recommendation. As a matter of course, the speech came as a bolt out of the blue to America's NATO allies. George Keyworth, the President's science adviser (and a Star Wars enthusiast), has said: 'This was not a speech that came up. It was a top-down speech . . . that came from the President's heart.' Or as General Haig put it less charitably, it came from the desire of the White House staff for a 'big PR splash that would make the President look like the greatest leader in America'.[7]

What was new in the President's project was its political (or ideological) aiming: the objective was no longer to be (as we had been told for twenty years) MAD (mutual assured destruction) but MAS (mutual assured security), to be performed by a technological fix. We will return to this. But there was, of course, nothing new about proposals for space weaponry or defences against ballistic missiles.

The story of all that would take us back thirty years, and we will not follow it in detail. Space has long been militarized: ICBMs pass through it, spy satellites orbit the globe, navigation, communications and control satellites have joined them, anti-satellite weapons (ASATs) have been tested, and the space shuttle regularly takes off on increasingly military missions.

The Soviet military have been quite as guilty as the American in pressing forward these developments. In one sense they bought Star Wars with the launching of the first space satellite, *Sputnik*, in October 1957, even though *Sputnik* was the innocent and well-advertised Soviet contribution to the International Geophysical Year. Even before the Soviet acquisition of the Bomb, they had invested intensively in long-range rocketry for geo-strategic reasons; in plain English, the American military could threaten to deliver nuclear weapons on to Soviet territory by bombers or by intermediate-range missiles from forward bases relatively close to the Soviet Union (such as the Thor, which was based in East Anglia but kept secret from the British people); whereas the Soviet military could not reach United States territory unless they could throw their weapons across the Atlantic. Hence the Soviet military poured resources into engineering wizardry with mega-rockets, capable of lofting all manner of shit into space.

Such triumphs were bound to encourage misunderstandings. A large part of the American public was persuaded that *Sputnik* was an orbiting bomb: or, if not yet a bomb, then the precursor of an orbiting platform from which the Commies would drop bombs on their heads. James Killian, an American scientific adviser at the time, writes:

As it beeped in the sky, *Sputnik I* created a crisis of confidence that swept the country like a windblown forest fire. Overnight there developed a widespread fear that the country lay at the mercy of the Russian military machine and that our own government and its military arm had abruptly lost the power to defend the mainland itself, much less to maintain US prestige and leadership in the international arena.[8]

Sputnik was not the only Soviet 'first'. On 12 April 1961, Yuri Gagarin was pitched aloft on the first manned orbital flight in *Vostok I*. The world's admiration at this astonishing exploit was a good deal lessened when it went to Khrushchev's head. Four months later, at a Kremlin reception in honour of the second astronaut, Titov, Khrushchev squared up to the Western imperialist aggressors and boasted:

> You do not have 50 and 100 megaton bombs. We have bombs stronger than 100 megatons. We placed Gagarin and Titov in space and we can replace them with other loads that can be directed to any place on earth.

These ugly (and baseless) menaces were part of the diplomatic play during the Berlin crisis of that year, but they were given added menace in February 1963 when Marshal Biriuzov, Chief of the Soviet Strategic Rocket Forces, declared: 'It has now become possible at a command from earth to launch missiles from satellites at any desired time and at any point in the satellite trajectory.'[9]

The threat of the orbiting bomb, or of the delivery of missiles from space – threats encouraged by this Soviet boasting – preoccupied the public mind in those years. Privately, American defence experts were less alarmed: 'A bomb could not be dropped from a satellite on a target below, because anything dropped from a satellite would simply continue alongside in orbit.' And a satellite 'will always be a poor choice' for launching a missile at the ground, since other (ground-, sea-, or air-based) means of delivery promised greater accuracy, throw-weight, etc.[10] The impracticality or inefficiency of space-based weapons was an argument which lubricated the successful conclusion of the Outer Space Treaty of 1967 (see p. 72) under which they are outlawed. Subsequently the orbiting bomb dropped out of discussion. Today there is speculation about earth-to-space and space-to-space weapons but less speculation about space-based weaponry directed at the earth (but see p. 131).

The alarm provoked among the American public by the Soviet space lead in the late 1950s and early 1960s led to a spurt in American space developments. But we enter here a thicket of hypocrisy too tangled to penetrate. In fact the United States armed forces – often in competition with each other – were plunging ahead with many devices. But these were subordinated to the politics of global public relations, in which successive Presidents sought to gain prestige by projecting the image of American commitment to 'the peaceful uses of space' – a cause which was to reach its climax with the superb success of the Apollo moon landing.

Hence all US military developments in space were shrouded in secrecy. And, as a sub-plot, the highest Pentagon advisers and the intelligence community cautioned against any over-reaction against Soviet satellites, since they wished to safeguard the right for their own military satellites to operate in space. In view of impenetrable Soviet secrecy on military questions, the United States military saw greater advantage to themselves in the uncontested use of 'spy' satellites – especially after the shooting-down of Gary Powers's U-2 high-altitude spy plane – than any that would be gained by their Soviet counterparts. By launching *Sputniks* the Russians had 'done us a good turn . . . in establishing the concept of freedom of international space'. But in order not to tarnish the public-relations image of America as the guardian of space as a sanctuary for peace, an official blackout was imposed upon any acknowledgement of the military uses of their own satellites. This hypocritical exercise in disinformation commenced in the Eisenhower years, was formally codified in 1962 under Kennedy, and remained operative until June 1978. The leaders of America's 'closest allies' were briefed as to the true military functions of the satellites, but only so that they could disinform their own publics and back up American diplomatic lies in the United Nations. The Russians, of course, knew what the satellites were up to, and matched them with their own. As an actor in these events has confessed: 'We were not fooling anybody except our own people.'[11]

In the intermediate years (the 1960s and 1970s) the United States developed an anti-satellite (ASAT) system, and then let it fall into obsolescence; experimented with other ASAT and BMD devices with happy names like SAINT, Dynasoar, BAMBI and Early Spring; and, more recently, developed and tested an advanced ASAT capability (p. 43); while the Soviet Union has proceeded, with only a brief interruption in the early 1970s, with developing and testing its own ASAT system, capable of low-orbit intercepts.

The development of active defences against ballistic missiles (BMD) also dates back, on both sides, to the 1950s. By the early 1960s in the United States there was a serious lobby to deploy a system (Nike-X) to defend fifty major cities. The proposal was vetoed by President Johnson in 1966. At about the same time a Soviet system (the Galosh) began to be deployed around Moscow. These systems depended upon nuclear-tipped precision missiles designed to explode in the upper atmosphere close to the terminal stage of incoming ICBMs. But even at this stage it was evident that counter-measures to trick or to penetrate defences could be evolved more swiftly and more cheaply than the ABM defences themselves. As two nuclear weapons experts noted: 'The practical fact is that work on defensive systems turns out to be the best way to promote invention of the penetration aids that nullify them.'[12]

For various reasons (costs and impracticality among them) these developments were checked in 1972 when the USA and USSR reached one of their rare agreements, the ABM Treaty, which mutually renounced all but two limited systems (and subsequently one) on each side. Whatever the true reasons for this unaccustomed accord, the treaty has been celebrated as the crowning moment of the Rule of Mutual Assured Destruction (MAD) – see Chapter 4. In order not to destabilize the balance of 'deterrence', both parties agreed to leave themselves exposed to the retaliation of the missiles of the other.

THE LOBBY FOR STAR WARS

Soon after this a new lobby arose which can be seen as the precursor of Star Wars. Pressures within the armed services for new ASAT developments were strengthened when the Soviet Union resumed ASAT testing in 1976; increasing accuracy of Soviet ICBMs renewed the demand for ABM defences of US missile silos; and more exotic experiments within the great aerospace contractors and research laboratories were in search of sponsors and budgetary back-up. By the end of Carter's presidency and the first years of Reagan's these pressures were reflected in upwards-creeping budgetary appropriations for space-related research and development. Already in 1982 the formal allocation for US Department of Defense space projects ($6.4 billion) had overtaken the supposedly peaceful budget of the National Aeronautics and Space Administration (NASA) at $5.9 billion; and since 49 per cent of NASA's space-shuttle flights are now for military purposes, the real position is understated. Moreover, the budget allocation for reconnaissance satellites is not included in these figures.[13]

These pressures were piecemeal: the thrust of various interest groups. What they lacked was an overall strategic and political rationale – the ideological glue to fix them together as one single lobby. In a sense, the greatest glue-finder was always Ronald Reagan himself. As Governor of California in the late 1960s he was a visitor to the Lawrence Livermore Laboratory, and he showed a layman's fascination with its exotic space researches. There commenced his association with Dr Edward Teller, the Laboratory's founder.

During the Republican presidential primary campaign in 1980, Reagan was shown around the North American Defense Command (NORAD), an arcane cavern inside a mountain in Colorado. He later told Robert Scheer:

NORAD is an amazing place . . . They actually are tracking several thousand objects in space, meaning satellites of ours and everyone else's, even down to the point that they are tracking a glove lost by an astronaut that is still circling the earth up there. I think the thing that struck me was the irony that here, with this great technology of ours, we can do all of this yet we cannot stop any of the weapons that are coming at us. I don't think there's been a time in history when there wasn't a defence against some kind of thrust, even back in the old-fashioned days when we had coast artillery that would stop invading ships if they came.

Mutual Assured Destruction (he told Scheer) 'was a ridiculous plan . . . based on the idea that the two countries would hold each other's population hostage, that we would not protect or defend our people against a nuclear attack'. He wanted to 'take a look at this', but 'I would have to have access to more information than I presently have.'[14]

Reagan's own launch-pad for the presidency was his home state of California, and in that sense he directly represents major centres of the space-related institutions and industries: the Lawrence Livermore Laboratory (a centre for charged-particle beam researches among much else); the US Air Force Space Division in El Segundo; the Vandenberg Air Force base, from which military shuttle flights take place, some fifty miles from Reagan's 'Western White House'; Rockwell's plant at Downey, engaged in major space-related research and contracting; and a dozen other contractors and scores of subcontractors. Undoubtedly this background influenced his campaigning strategy, which included proposals for ballistic-missile defences alongside a military build-up in every possible field.[15]

Once elected President, Reagan had access to whatever information he called for. He was already disposed to call for what he wanted to hear. Some of his information came from lobbyists and think-tanks of the alarmist Right. Pressures came from Republican opponents of all arms-control agreements, from the Livermore Laboratory, and from the Herz Foundation, which has funded space research; and, from 1981, from a group of influential scientists, industrialists, military men and aerospace executives meeting regularly at the Heritage Foundation in Washington, with experience in lobbying the White House and Congress.

Dr Edward Teller keeps appearing in this story. A Hungarian by birth, he fled Nazi Germany in the thirties and later took part in the Manhattan Project to develop the A-bomb. He appears to remain transfixed within the traumatic moments of the first Cold War, when, in a notorious episode, he testified against Oppenheimer for his lack of 'moral support' for the development of the H-bomb. A recent visitor found him to be a vehement anti-Communist, obsessed with Soviet expansionism, the dangers of Western 'appeasement' and of Nicaraguan Sandinistas, and with the need for military build-up. To dispute any of these points was 'like arguing about family relations with King Lear'.[16] Teller founded, and still presides over, the Livermore Laboratory, and is a member of the group that met at the Heritage Foundation. Reagan selected as his personal science advisor Dr George Keyworth, a nuclear physicist strongly supported by Dr Teller.

Teller's own role was a good deal more than advisory. He was, and is, a prominent publicist of the case for enhancing America's nuclear strength, writing in alarmist terms about Soviet strategic 'superiority' and in opposition to the Freeze movement. Moreover, he and his associates at Livermore were working on a neat new device: the X-ray laser. The principles of this device were successfully tested beneath the Nevada desert on 14 November 1980, and Teller acclaimed this as the decisive breakthrough, of equal significance to the invention of A- and H-bombs – a 'third generation' weapon. This nuclear X-ray laser combat station (see pp. 31–5) is envisaged as an elaborate bomb placed in space orbit which, when detonated, would pump out multiple laser beams aimed along rods at predetermined targets before the whole thing burned itself up in a ball of fire.

Edward Teller rode high on the X-ray laser in 1982 and 1983, when the President was getting his briefings; he was selling it as the ultimate technological fix. Such weapons (he later informed the President), by converting hydrogen bombs into hitherto unprecedented forms and by directing these in highly effective fashions against enemy targets would end the MAD era and commence a period of assured survival on terms favourable to the Western alliance.[17]

Even admirers among his scientific colleagues were less than certain. 'The X-ray laser was elegant,' one said:

But is Edward an engineer? No. Is he a systems designer? No. Is he a military planner? No. He was enthralled with the principle and rightly so. The principle is in fact that beautiful. But he is not the kind of guy that ever got hooked on building things. His first H-bomb was the size of an apartment house. Edward is a physicist with a fantastic creative mind. He understands the beauty of a piece of music. But for God's sake don't ask him to design a trumpet.[18]

Those who admired Dr Teller a little less noted other objections. His former colleague, the eminent physicist and Nobel Laureate Hans A. Bethe, began to raise an opposition. Such orbiting combat stations could be easily destroyed or outwitted by counter-measures. It was noted that nuclear detonations in space, devoid of atmospheric resistance, would rock or destroy any communications satellites in that sector. A group of eminent Soviet scientists made a more tight-lipped objection:

The possibility of aiming rods at targets and keeping the assigned direction under the action of a nuclear explosion is far from being apparent.[19]

Such objections did not disturb the influential group meeting at the Heritage Foundation. These included Dr Teller, several members of the President's own 'kitchen cabinet' – Joseph Coors, a beer emperor, Justin Dart, a wealthy businessman, and Jacquelin Hume, an industrialist – and a former Under-Secretary of the Army, Karl R. Bendetsen, an old friend of Teller's who was also chairman of the board of Champion International Corporation and a director of the (ferociously Cold War) Hoover Institute on War, Revolution, and Peace. Also prominent was Lieutenant-General Daniel O. Graham, a former head of the Defense Intelligence Agency.

By the end of 1981 this group split into two. The ins and outs of this division need not concern us much, since it is important that *both* groups continued to influence the President. Teller's half of the group (with the President's 'kitchen cabinet' in tow) emphasized basic research and development – with third-generation nuclear weapons prominent – carried out through national laboratories, academic institutes and research contractors. They had several meetings with the President in the run-up to the Star Wars speech, and Dr Teller had at least one private audience at which he argued that ABMs would not only defend missile silos but might make possible a defence of the entire American nation. Immediately after the Star Wars speech Dr Teller rushed forward with acclaim: 'Mr Reagan did not lightly accept the idea that these [systems] can be made to work. He wanted to know a vast number of details. He asked questions . . . of many scientists, myself included. He then decided that something must and can be done.'[20]

The other faction of the Heritage group was led by General Graham. Having less direct access to the President, Graham formed a public lobby called High Frontier. He represented more directly the interests of aerospace and high-tech contractors impatient to get on with profitable applications, and pushing for the early deployment of ABM systems of a limited kind and the ending of treaty limitations. He called publicly for 'a technological end-run on the Soviets'. High Frontier raised half a million dollars from private right-wing sources for its research and publicity in 1981-2, and put forward the proposal for a three-layered defence (see p. 30). Graham also argued for the replacement of MAD (mutual assured destruction) with the strategy of 'assured survivability for the United States'.[21] Although the High Frontier proposals were investigated by the Pentagon and also by the Congressional Office of Technology Assessment and were rejected by both, this did not discourage the President. He continued to cite the High Frontier report, which he evidently found to be ideologically nutritious, with its space-fic diagrams, its elaborate layered defences and its homely promise of MAS.

That is how Star Wars was conceived, and how the speech came about.

PUTTING DOWN THE MX

That is not, of course, the full story. If one is a very great man, and the President of the greatest nation on earth, one has to make do with genius and intuition when lesser mortals would have the opportunity to spend months in study. And, also, one is being bombarded by hundreds of other preoccupations which arrive on one's desk simultaneously.

One has to turn over a great many things in one's mind while chopping wood back on the ranch.

Among all these preoccupations, there are two which may have focused the President's attention on space defence. The first was the problem of that blasted M X missile. This lovely big missile, with its ten accurate warheads, was inherited by Reagan from President Carter.

The M X missile – if anyone can still remember – was originally planned to occupy a 6,000-square-mile complex in Nevada and Utah, with 10,000 miles of roadway, and with missile-tracks which would move through elaborate loops between 4,600 case-hardened shelters. The missiles were to be hidden as in a shell-game, like a pea under thimbles. Most of the missile-carriers on the tracks were to be empty dummies (whose tops, however, were to be opened for a short while every day for inspection by Soviet satellites to show that the missiles had not reproduced like rabbits in the night). Then the carriers would disappear into hangars, and the real missiles would be shuffled around so that the Russians could never know which carrier was which. It was calculated that the whole project would be the greatest and most expensive single human artefact known to civilization – or, more properly, to barbarism.

The loyal populace of Utah and Nevada did not find this funny. The project aroused universal dislike. A columnist in *The New York Times*, Mr Russell Baker, proposed that it would be cheaper – and would fox the Russians even more – if a number of dummy Pentagons could be built and moved around the US road-system along with the real Pentagon every day. What could the Russians do *then*?

Reagan had to find some other home for this lovely missile. But he found that his own alarmist electioneering propaganda had blown up in his face. In order to stampede the American people into approving his heavy military appropriations he and fellow Republican candidates in the 1980 election had made great play with the notion of a 'window of vulnerability'. This notion as to the threat which Soviet I CBMs posed to US missile silos had been peddled by some wild-eyed ideologues of worst-case analysis in the 'defence community', taken to the public by hired P R men, and taken up by the Committee on the Present Danger – the formidable right-wing pressure-group which campaigned against SALT II and for Reagan's election.

The 'window of vulnerability' was intended to scare Americans into supposing that there was a hole in their skies – a hole left there by the negligence of President Carter – through which they might expect Soviet ICBMs to enter at any moment. This was because of the increasing accuracy of Soviet ballistic missiles. The Soviets might now – maybe not today but tomorrow – launch a first strike which would take out all the Minutemen in their silos, hence disarming America and making retaliation impossible. All that the Soviets need do would be to ground-burst two nuclear warheads of one megaton each with perfect accuracy on each silo (1,000 in the case of the Minutemen). Easy! Already, the soon-to-be President warned, the window might be so wide open that 'the Russians could just take us with a phone call'. 'Hallo! Mr Reagan, is zat you? Tovarich Brezhnev here. Come on out with your hands up, or I put zis Bomb through ze window!'

Middle America was shit-scared and rushed to help the Republicans with hammers in their hands and nails between their teeth. The window must be boarded up! But the way to do this, it seemed, was not with boards but by pointing MX missiles at the window, and placing them so cleverly (in dense packs or on air-patrol or in case-hardened silos) that the incoming ICBMs could not hope to get them, and would fly away in despair.

All this alarmist electioneering was as mendacious as had been Kennedy's self-induced panic about a 'missile gap' in 1960. The US 'deterrent' had long been based upon a triad – missiles deployed on land, in the air and at sea – and the worst-case analysts could only pretend that one leg out of the three was at risk. (In fact, the Soviet 'deterrent', which relies more heavily on land-based ICBMs, could be argued more convincingly to be at risk to a disarming first strike.)

But as soon as the President was elected he found that he had bought a problem for himself. The MX shell-game had been rejected. The public had laughed it out of existence, and it also had, in Reagan's eyes, the overwhelming drawback of having been prepared by President Carter. Yet every other proposal for MX-basing was criticized – by the zealous adherents of his own 'window of vulnerability' gospel.

If he was to put the MX into the holes vacated by ailing and elderly Titans – holes which the Soviet military had presumably long noticed and targeted – then he was putting them right under the window. Nothing in the President's first administration gave him more head-aches than his tussle, both with Congress and with the American public, around MX. At one stage it seemed probable that the Freeze movement would halt the project altogether; only the providential shooting-down of the Korean airliner, KAL 007, enabled Reagan to push his appropriations through a shocked Congress.[22]

The problem of protecting MX missiles – of boarding up the window above them – was a significant catalyst for President Reagan's interest in Star Wars. The US Army had proposed a new Low Altitude Defense (LoAD) system, but this was found to be too leaky and was dropped, in 1982, in favour of a projected Baseline Terminal Defense (BTD). Both defences depended upon launching ground-to-air missiles to detonate small nuclear warheads in the vicinity of enemy ICBMs as they were homing in – i.e entering the window. But the idea fell out of favour with the government's own advisers: 'If we want to spend money on things that go bang, then maybe we should spend it on things that go bang over the Soviet Union and not us.'

The debate on MX basing and defences focused attention on two problems which led towards Star Wars. First, defences against ICBMs must be extended right through the whole arc of their flight, from the moment of blast-off, and not be confined to their terminal phase. Hence they must be carried into space, and, in Caspar Weinberger's words, 'engage ballistic missiles and warheads along their entire launch-to-impact trajectories'.[23] Second, both the military and the administration were stubbing their toes repeatedly against the limits imposed by the ABM Treaty of 1972. As early as 1980, Richard Burt, then writing alarmist articles in *The New York Times* and subsequently appointed by Mr Reagan to the post of Under-Secretary of State for European Affairs, wrote that 'revision of the ABM Treaty to facilitate the deployment of hard-site missile defences is an especially interesting option . . . It might even rule out the need for deceptive basing modes [for MX] altogether, by giving fixed silos a new lease on life.' In December 1982, giving evidence to the Senate Armed Services Committee in favour of the 'dense pack' system of MX basing, Caspar Weinberger proposed that 'we could put an ABM system' to defend the proposed dense pack at Fort Warren, Wyoming. Weinberger made it clear that he was fully prepared to notify the USSR of his 'revision' (in fact, breach) of the ABM Treaty 'anytime it is determined that an ABM system is constructed'.[24]

PUTTING DOWN THE PEACE MOVEMENT

All this the President turned over in his mind, down on the ranch chopping his wood. But what he came up with startled everyone. This may have been because a second preoccupation was buzzing around in his head. He was bothered, just at that time, not only about getting MX through Congress, but also about bishops. Whenever he looked inside his head he found a bishop and an MX missile there, quarrelling with each other. There was no way in which he could get them to agree. If he found a nice place to put down the missile, the bishop ran up with his crozier and knocked it over. If he tried to please the bishop, then there was no way at all of putting down the MX.

The President was bothered not only about bishops, of course, but also about the huge inroads being made in his hitherto loyal Republican constituency by the burgeoning American peace movement. Once again, the alarmist notes sounded in his election campaign and his first years in office had blown up in his own face.

We have to explain that the United States is very much like an island, although you will know (if you have been there) that it is somewhat larger than one has come to expect of islands. If you look at a map you will find that there is a large amount of water on each side of it, which waters are called the Atlantic and Pacific oceans. The United States has grown up from its cradle, secure in the immunity from invasion provided by these oceans. Apart from the time when British gunboats burned down Washington, and apart from their own civil war, Americans have been accustomed to think of real wars as being 'over there'. And, in 1983, President Reagan had not yet thought to warn them that they were in imminent danger of being overrun by revolutionary hordes from Nicaragua.

Hence the American people had slumbered comfortably in their security until Reagan himself awoke them roughly in his election campaign of 1980, when he informed them that their armed forces were in a state of decay, the Soviets had overtaken them and acquired superiority, and that at any time Soviet ICBMs might come in through the window.

The effect upon the complacency of the uninformed 'average' citizen in Middle America was shattering. It was not what the President had intended. They understood for the first time that US territory was not sacrosanct and that they were themselves directly in the nuclear target area. A survey taken by the Public Agenda Foundation in 1984 reveals a quite remarkable turn-around in national responses: 96 per cent of the sample believe that 'picking a fight with the Soviet Union is too dangerous in a nuclear world' and 89 per cent that 'both the USA and the USSR would be completely destroyed' in an all-out nuclear war; indeed, 83 per cent – who had by then followed the reports on the nuclear winter – said that 'we cannot be certain that life on earth will continue after a nuclear war'.[25]

This sudden sense of insecurity undoubtedly contributed to the strength of the American Freeze movement, and to the astonishing speed with which it spread. Arising in 1981, by November 1982 the tide had reached the point where the Freeze had been placed as an issue on the ballot of eleven states and had been carried in all but one. Among the states voting 'yes' to the Freeze was the President's own California, and the states involved contained over a quarter of the population of the USA. Senators and Congresspersons were receiving heavy postbags from their constituents and, in consequence, were voting against certain military appropriations. Opinion polls showed a majority for the Freeze among Republican voters.

What was at issue was the 'credibility' of nuclear deterrence. For the Freeze movement was much more than a surge of insecurity. It was organized and made articulate by a staunch peace movement – indeed, scores of different movements speaking in differing accents – with internationalist conscience and tough moral concern. A strong motive was not only fear of being nuked but also a refusal of the immorality of threatening to nuke other equally defenceless people. And one of the most influential and unequivocal statements of this refusal came in the form of a carefully argued pastoral letter discussed by the conference of Roman Catholic bishops in Washington in November 1982.

This was not a casual pronouncement. It was attentive to both strategic and theological issues:

> The moral issue at stake in nuclear war involves the meaning of sin in its most graphic dimensions ... Today the destructive potential of the nuclear powers threatens the sovereignty of God over the world he has brought into being. We could destroy his work.

The letter rejected the quest for superiority, and condemned any use of threat or of first strike: 'the danger of escalation is so great that it is an unacceptable moral risk to initiate nuclear war in any form'. While the bishops stopped just short of condemning the doctrine of deterrence, they could accept it only as 'a step on the way toward progressive disarmament'. Should this condition not be met, then the moral attitude of the Church 'would certainly have to shift to one of uncompromising condemnation of both use and possession of such weapons'.

This letter ambushed President Reagan from an unexpected quarter. He could not brush aside the Catholic bishops, nor, indeed, the multitude of his own supporters who were endorsing the Freeze, as a bunch of Commies. He had supposed that he was the nation's specialist in moral homilies, but here were competitors who could threaten his sovereignty over the world he had brought into being, and who could destroy his work. All this was preoccupying the President's mind in the first months of 1983.

We should explain that the first duty of a President is not to ensure the security of the nation but to ensure the security of his own political future. This duty was uppermost in President Reagan's mind at that time, since he had recently decided that he would run for a second term. And now the bishops and all those Freezers were getting in the way. How could he put the MX down *and* put the bishops down at the same time, and also get himself re-elected, when the Democrats were trying to steal his voters off him by supporting the Freeze?

It was while pondering these dilemmas that the President was illuminated by The Force. He recalled his briefings from the Heritage and High Frontier circles. He recalled his monthly meetings with the Joint Chiefs of Staff, who were pressing for a reconsideration of BMD cover for the MX and other missile sites.[26] (Already in early 1982 Pentagon officials were calling the US Army's ballistic-missile defence programme 'the hottest game in town'.)[27] He recalled his discussions with Edward Teller and with Senator Harrison H. Schmitt – a former astronaut and chairman of the Senate Subcommittee on Science, Technology and Space – on the use of laser weapons for strategic defence.[28] He stirred all these ingredients together in a solution of lay infatuation with exotic technology, and tipped into the mixture his own long antipathy to MAD. And he mixed a potion that was strong enough to poison the Soviets and to poison the peace movement at the same time.

So the President flew back to Washington, where he made a very beautiful speech, some part of which he is even rumoured to have written himself.[29] He offered to change the course of history, and to provide new hope for our children in the twenty-first century. The very idea of deterrence through the threat of retaliation was 'immoral'. He out-homilied the bishops and he stole the Freeze movement's clothes while it was bathing. 'The human spirit must be capable of rising above dealing with other nations and human beings by threatening their existence.'

What if free people could live secure in the knowledge that their security did not rest upon the threat of instant US retaliation to deter a Soviet attack; that we could intercept and destroy strategic ballistic missiles before they reached our own soil or that of our allies? . . .

I call upon the scientific community who gave us nuclear weapons to turn their great talents to the cause of mankind and world peace: to give us the means of rendering these nuclear weapons impotent and obsolete.

He offered the perturbed citizens of Middle America an impermeable shield far more secure than the Freeze. He wrested the moral crozier from the bishops and regained the high ground of idealism: 'Wouldn't it be better to save lives than to avenge them?' The speech was as homely as American apple pie and it went down big.

It was, truly, a speech of genius in the great tradition of oratory of Elmer Gantry. Europeans commonly underestimate President Reagan, and mistake the tradition to which he belongs. His genius is not that of originality or profundity of any kind. He is not a thinker nor a strategist nor an energetic administrator nor a bureaucratic fixer. He is not even well-informed. His genius is that of a 'Communicator': that is, he is a media-projector, and the alpha product of a consumer society with sophisticated techniques of salesmanship and public relations. He is the front man, projected by the media, and supported by an elaborate sales and PR organization. But he is more than that. His gift as a Communicator lies in his ultra-sensitive sensors to detect what the Middle American public *wish* to be told – to emit homely, comforting, moralizing or inspiriting noises which set their deepest prejudices vibrating in sympathy with his rhetoric – to justify, promote and sell any policy by aiming it unerringly at the lowest common denominator of inherited responses. In short his genius is as a populist ideologist. The Star Wars speech – and its successors – comforted a lot of people, and made them feel both patriotic and altruistic about spending billions more dollars on military adventures.

At first the speech had the Pentagon and the State Department spinning in confusion. Confusion was short-lived. Allegiance to the speech was imposed on all the entourage of power like 'a loyalty oath'. The President's credibility might not be questioned and enthusiasm for Star Wars became the path to promotion. Critics were reduced to making snide, off-the-record, unattributed one-liners: 'This is the President's programme. We can't tell the President he's got a nutty idea.' Or (from a disgruntled scientist at NASA): 'He grew up with all those old Buck Rogers flicks. I guess we're stuck with it.' [30]

As for America's NATO allies, at first they smirked incredulously behind their hands, or yawned, or put it down to the adolescence of the political system in Washington. So also did the European peace movements, preoccupied in 1983 with the more terrestrial issues of oncoming cruise and Pershing missiles. That is why Star Wars crept up on us by stealth. It was only after the President's re-election and his inaugural in which SDI was given new priority, that Europe sat up with a jerk. Good God, the man is in earnest! Throughout the assemblies of Europe the cry went up: *What is Star Wars?*

2 · What is Star Wars?

Ben Thompson

Once rockets go up who cares where they come down.
'That's not my department' says Wernher von Braun.

Tom Lehrer

The Strategic Defence Initiative, or 'Star Wars' as it has affectionately come to be known, proposes the erection of a full-scale anti-ballistic-missile defence, described variously as being capable of partially, almost completely, or perfectly neutralizing a nuclear attack from the direction of the Soviet Union, or possibly from a smaller nuclear power. The cost of putting such a system into operation has been estimated at one thousand billion dollars or more (cf. $25 billion for the Apollo Moon project). Since this notion was formally proposed by President Reagan it has been the subject of considerable research, speculation and lobbying from scientific, social, and commercial interest groups, and as a result certain modifications of tone have become apparent in the way in which SDI is now being presented. In particular, the US administration seems to have responded to widespread scepticism concerning the possibility of a completely impenetrable anti-missile defence by reducing emphasis on this possibility and stressing instead the expected commercial and scientific benefits of SDI. However this change of attitude has apparently been made for the benefit of policy-makers rather than the public, with the result that the popular image of 'Star Wars' has become confused and unclear. Will it make nuclear weapons 'impotent and obsolete'? Will it protect Europeans or only Americans? Will it protect anyone at all?

AN OUTLINE OF SPACE DEFENCE SYSTEMS

Since the development of the first ground-launched ballistic missiles in the 1960s, the possibility of mounting a successful defence against ballistic missile attack has been considered and researched upon in the laboratories of the superpowers. In 1972 the ABM Treaty was signed and ratified by both superpowers. This treaty explicitly forbids the deployment or field testing of anti-ballistic-missile defence (ABM) systems except in certain very limited cases. Initially both parties were allowed to construct two ABM systems (later revised to one), which were to be immobile and subject to various constraints, at sites of their choice. The Russians built a primitive ABM system around Moscow while the Americans built an ABM system to defend a missile silo field at Grand Forks, North Dakota. The US subsequently dismantled their system, partly because they realized that its nuclear-tipped interceptors would cause unacceptable havoc with their own communications systems. The Russians kept their system, and are believed to be still updating and improving it. The Russian system is nevertheless not regarded by American defence experts as sufficiently sophisticated to offer serious resistance to a US nuclear strike against Moscow.[1]

A parallel and related question is that of anti-satellite warfare (ASAT). The ABM Treaty does not ban ASAT research and testing, though interference with each other's surveillance satellites is explicitly forbidden, since the satellites provide the major means for verification of the treaty. However, both sides undertake:

Not to give missiles, launchers, or radars, other than ABM interceptor missiles, ABM launchers or ABM radars, capabilities to counter strategic ballistic missiles or their elements in flight trajectory, and not to test them in ABM mode.[2]

All 'Star Wars' concepts depend heavily on prepositioned satellites, both as ABM weapons and as sensors, data processors and transmitters. Problems of ASAT and complimentary DSAT (satellite defence) are therefore important to these ideas. It is clear that much research and testing in this area is becoming very hard to distinguish from ABM activity and is therefore bringing the ABM Treaty under attack even at this stage. We will come back to this.

THE THEORY OF STAR WARS

The Three-layer Principle

All previous ABM systems relied upon a single principle, that of physically destroying or disabling the attacking ballistic missile warheads as they re-enter the earth's atmosphere from space over their targets. The key element in SDI is the proposal that Russian missile boosters could be attacked while they were rising through the atmosphere from their silos and at the stage when the individual warheads had not yet been released. A second layer of interceptors could then tackle those warheads which had evaded destruction by the first layer, leaving a final layer of interceptors, similar to the original ABM interceptors, to deal with any warheads which managed to re-enter the atmosphere over their targets. The theory is that these layers would have a cumulative defensive effect. For example, if each layer was 90 per cent 'leakproof' then the system as a whole would be virtually hermetic. Only 10 per cent of 10 per cent of 10 per cent would get through the defence as a whole, leaving 0.1 per cent of the total number of warheads launched arriving on target.

However, the success of this approach depends vitally upon the success of the first layer of the defence, the so-called 'boost-phase' layer, which would disable a proportion of the ascending ICBMs before they had a chance to release their multiple warheads along with any accompanying decoy devices. This is because the second-stage defence, interception in space or 'mid-course interception', absolutely depends upon the limitation of the number of real or potential threats which it faces. We shall examine the particular problems of each layer and the systems proposed for their defence below.

Boost-phase Defence

Intercontinental ballistic missiles of current design take between three and five minutes to climb through the earth's atmosphere, burn out their fuel and release their cargo of warheads and decoys in space. Current Russian designs are slower in this respect than American designs. The MX missile completes its boost phase in about three minutes, as against five minutes for the liquid-fuelled Russian SS 18. During these few minutes a 'Star Wars' boost-phase defence would have to be alerted, manoeuvre itself into a position to attack, power itself up and respond with perfect accuracy and reliability to the rising missile boosters. It would need to do this despite any counter-measures that might be directed against it and regardless of prevailing weather conditions, radio interference or contingencies of attack pattern chosen. In the case of orbiting defences, sufficient forces would have to be on orbit and in working order so that whatever moment was chosen for the attack enough satellites would be within range of the Russian missile silos to intercept all their boosters even if launched simultaneously. Because of the short reaction time available much attention has been given to the possibility of using Luke-Skywalker-like beam weapons which could either be based in orbit or, according to another plan, could direct their power from earth to large orbiting mirrors which would then redirect the power, perhaps via smaller mirrors, towards the ascending boosters. Three types of beam weapons have mainly figured in these discussions, chemical lasers, X-ray lasers and particle-beam weapons.

(i) Chemical Lasers

LASER means 'light amplification by stimulated emission of radiation'. In a chemical laser, energy is pumped into the molecules of a gas or crystal in such a way that they can be stimulated into giving up all their energy at once in a sort of chain reaction or cascade. The resulting light has several special properties. It is extremely 'coherent', meaning that the troughs and crests of the light waves emerging from the lasing medium are all perfectly aligned, in contrast with the light from an ordinary source such as a light bulb where the light waves are randomly out of phase with each other. (It is this property of laser light which is used to make holograms.) This means that a lot of power can be packed into a laser beam, and also that such a beam can be very finely focused over long distances. A laser rangefinder currently in use by the Royal Greenwich Observatory can measure the distance to a satellite so accurately that it has detected variations of milliseconds in the length of a day due to imbalances in the trade winds.[3] However, the most powerful lasers currently in existence are of the order of 100 to 1,000 times weaker than those which would be needed to attack a rocket booster.

According to the SDI concept of laser weapons, three possible ways of basing the lasers are considered. The first method is to base the lasers permanently in space. According to this plan battle stations would be lifted on the space shuttle, or some type of mass-cargo space vehicle, or built in earth orbit from components lifted into orbit on such vehicles. Stations would either be placed in a geostationary orbit (that is, so high up that they orbit the earth in the same period that the earth itself rotates), where they would remain permanently over the Russian missile silos, or in a lower orbit where they would trade off the need to deploy more battle stations for proximity to the ascending boosters. More battle stations would need to be deployed in the second case, because satellites in a low orbit circle the earth every few hours, so enough satellites have to be put up to cover for those which are out of sight of their targets at any one time.

A second method, one favoured by George Keyworth, President Reagan's scientific adviser, is to base the lasers on mountain peaks and beam their rays up to large relay mirrors in geostationary orbits. These mirrors would then beam power to a collection of smaller mirrors in lower orbits which would pick off the individual ICBM boosters in quick succession. This method has the attraction that extra lasers do not need to be built to compensate for absent satellites, and that the vulnerable lasers and their large and expensive power sources are safely on the ground. However, even on mountain peaks lasers would be vulnerable to weather conditions, cloud cover, etc., meaning that extra lasers would need to be constructed in compensation.

The third method of basing being considered for lasers and other 'Star Wars' systems is the 'pop-up' method. The weapons would be kept on the ground until such time as they were needed. The problem with this idea is that because the earth is round, any pop-up weapon would have to climb to a certain height simply in order to see its target over the horizon. The pop-up booster would therefore have to accelerate many times faster than the missiles that it was attacking in order to fire off its weapons before the target booster completed its launch. Pop-up systems based on the United States would be separated by about 90° of arc from the Russian silo fields. They would thus require rocket launchers several thousand times larger than the rocket which took the Apollo astronauts to the moon. An alternative basing mode would be to try and put the pop-up boosters in Europe (see p. 123), but even so, enormous boosters and computerized instant-launch systems would be needed to ensure even a few seconds' glimpse of the target over the horizon. If the pop-ups were based at sea they could be nearer the missile fields, but they would then become vulnerable to a disabling anti-submarine strike. To be sure of success, submarines would need to hover permanently in the vicinity of the Soviet Union, possibly accompanied by large protective convoys. In order to accommodate boosters powerful enough to launch the pop-ups, the submarines would have to be enormous; as one commentator put it, 'You pretty quickly reach the ridiculous state where the ocean isn't deep enough to hide the submarine, even when it's sitting on the bottom.'[4]

Laser defence schemes imply a staggering amount of investment, and the principles upon which they are based are still a long way from being realized in practice. Calculations by the Union of Concerned Scientists show that construction of a space-based laser defence would require the lifting of some 1,300 tons of laser fuel into space. And this is calculated using assumptions which some might feel were unreasonably favourable, i.e. perfect laser mirrors, lasers of optimum efficiency, and, perhaps most optimistic of all, the assumption that the Russians have simply maintained their current missile force as it is today! Even under these conditions the cost of simply lifting the battle stations into orbit would be of the order of $4 billion.[5] Kosta Tsipsis of the Massachusetts Institute of Technology estimates that, using ten space shuttles each flying three missions per year, it would still take between 3,200 and 6,400 years just to lift the fuels for a fleet of laser battle stations into orbit.[6] All such figures are highly speculative, but they give an idea of the size of the problem involved. Aside from the effectiveness of various forms of counter-measures, which we will discuss, these systems give a very poor return in terms of offence and defence, which is to say that the addition of relatively cheap ICBMs or even decoy ICBMs to the Russian armoury can force the deployment of inefficiently large numbers of American satellites to counter them.

Ground-based lasers suffer from similar problems of cost. Although not requiring to be lifted into orbit, the amount of power which must be generated is higher by a factor of three to ten due to the absorption of the laser light by the atmosphere. In order to provide sufficient power to deal with an attack of the size considered above, something between 100,000 and 300,000 megawatts of electric power would be needed. This represents between 20 and 60 per cent of the entire domestic power output of the United States! It would be impossible to extract this amount of power from the national grid, therefore specially designed power plants would have to be constructed at a cost of hundreds of billions of dollars. In order to overcome distortions of the laser beam due to fluctuating turbulence in the atmosphere (i.e. twinkling) the ground-based laser would be primed by a smaller laser based next to its mirror in space orbit. This technique, known as 'adaptive optics', has already been partly implemented in some modern astronomical telescopes, which use mirrors constructed of several segments which are kept in perfect alignment under computer control. In the case of a laser mirror the requirements would be especially stringent because the ground station would have to analyse the wavefront of the beam from the space-based 'beacon' laser and adapt the form of the transmitting mirror in a fraction of a second before the pattern of turbulence in the atmosphere could change. In order for the ground-based laser station to deliver its full power to the relays, the accuracy of the mirror would have to be maintained to within the order of one wavelength of the laser light (about one millionth of a centimetre for an ultraviolet laser). This level of accuracy would have to be maintained by all the mirrors in the chain, despite the large amounts of energy which they were redirecting. Small local variations in the form of the mirror, which would cause only minor aberrations in an astronomical mirror, rapidly absorb heat from the laser beam, leading quickly to severe distortion of the surface or destruction of the mirror.

However, assuming that the laser power can be generated, the problems are not over. The beam has to be directed on to the rocket booster with an accuracy of one or two yards over a distance of several thousand kilometres and held in position without moving or wavering for a period of seconds while it does its work. The target booster would be detected by the large amount of infra-red (heat) radiation emitted from its rocket motors. However, the rocket plume is not the same as the body of the rocket, and some form of active sensor like radar, but more probably a form of laser radar, would be needed to guide the beam. Both the infra-red detector and the radar would be susceptible to interference, blinding, creation of false signals, etc. In addition, because infra-red radiation has a longer wavelength than the beam of the laser itself, a mirror of around ten times the diameter of the laser mirror and ground to the same relative accuracy would be needed to aim the beam with the necessary precision.

Finally, it is still by no means certain when lasers of the required size can be built, if in fact they can be built at all. SDI analysts talk in terms of using 25 megawatt lasers in space, or ground-based lasers with power outputs in the 400-megawatts-plus range. However the most powerful US Airforce lasers now in existence produce an output of only about 400,000 watts and the Fletcher Commission has called for the demonstration of a 2-megawatt laser by 1987. It often happens in science (as indeed in other fields), that what appears to be simply a quantitative leap turns out to be a qualitative one. In the 1960s scientists were talking about the imminence of cheap renewable energy supplies from fusion power. However, a quarter of a century later so little progress has been made that both our own government and the US government are cutting back fusion research substantially. Interestingly enough, the root of the problem appears somewhat similar to the problem of developing military lasers, i.e. the problem of containing and usefully focusing huge amounts of power.

(ii) Particle Beams

Particle beams are related to the beams produced by large particle accelerators in the laboratory for research into the nature of atomic and sub-atomic matter. They suffer from serious drawbacks as far as SDI is concerned, and therefore don't require much discussion in the present state of the art. The chief drawback to particle beams seems to be that the manner in which they would interfere with the target is imprecise. Hopes seem to centre on the disruptive effect of the beam on the electronic circuits in the missile guidance system or possibly, at somewhat higher energies, the detonation of conventional high explosive in a nuclear warhead. A further serious drawback of particle beams is that they are curved by the earth's magnetic field in a way which makes them impossible to aim. A neutral particle beam can be produced which is not affected in this way, but as soon as it encounters even a trace of the earth's atmosphere it acquires a charge and spirals out of alignment.

Although particle beams appear at present to be unlikely candidates for boost-phase defence, some commentators believe that they may be used for terminal-defence systems in conjunction with lasers. This is based on the observation that under some conditions it may be possible to use a laser to create a 'tunnel' in the atmosphere which not only allows a particle beam to pass but may even help to focus and concentrate the beam. Scientists at Lawrence Livermore Laboratory have recently made cryptic hints about success in experiments with such a system. These weapons are, however, unlikely to appear in the first generation of SDI hardware if it ever arrives.

(iii) The X-ray Laser

The X-ray laser, as proposed by Dr Edward Teller, has a fundamentally different mode of operation from the other beam weapons so far discussed in that it derives its energy from a nuclear bomb. Scientists at Lawrence Livermore have shown that under the right conditions energy from a nuclear explosion can be pumped into a lasing material causing a short but extremely bright burst of laser radiation at X-ray wavelengths. Although X-rays are not reflected by mirrors in the same way as light beams are, the beam can be focused by careful design of the lasing rods. It turns out that because of the way in which the chain reaction of laser amplification takes place, a higher proportion of the laser energy is emitted from the ends of a rod of laser material than from the sides. By forming the lasing material into long thin fibres of the appropriate dimensions it is possible to focus the beam of X-rays over an area of a few hundred yards at a range of about 2,500 miles. At this range an X-ray laser might have enough power to damage a booster, and could probably knock it off course enough to protect a 'hard' target such as a missile silo which requires a very accurate hit.

The mechanism of the X-ray laser is quite different in principle from that of the chemical laser. Since the power is delivered in such a short burst (about a millionth of a second), the laser does not have to track the booster (indeed it would be unable to do so since it would no longer exist), and the large focusing area of the X-rays would make aiming somewhat less crucial. The laser burst is delivered instantaneously and the X-rays are absorbed into the first fraction of a millimetre of the booster skin, creating a shock wave which could damage the booster. The advantage of the X-ray laser is that the weapon itself would be very light in proportion to the amount of power that it delivered and, requiring no bulky power source, it might be cheaper and easier to lift into orbit. A laser battle station might be equipped with several sets of lasing rods in order to attempt to strike several separate targets with the energy from a single nuclear explosion. However, an X-ray-laser battle station would still require the same elaborate equipment for sensing and aiming at a target, which could more than nullify these advantages, particularly in the case of a laser intended to strike at more than one target at once.

There are further problems with the X-ray laser. A most serious technical problem is the fact that X-rays are strongly absorbed by air and cannot therefore attack boosters until they rise clear of the earth's atmosphere. In fact the energy from an X-ray laser could not be delivered to a rocket booster at a lower altitude than about sixty-five miles, which makes counter-defence against them quite easy, as we shall see later.

(iv) Kinetic-energy Weapons in Boost-phase Defence

A final possibility which is under investigation as a possible boost-phase defence are the so-called 'kinetic-energy weapons', i.e. rockets and electrically accelerated projectiles designed to bump into other rockets. These have the advantage that the technology is to a certain extent understood. However, the speed at which rockets and other kinetic-energy weapons would need to operate in order to intercept a booster in flight would prove a great disadvantage. Kinetic-energy weapons find their target by means of a mixture of infra-red sensors and radar, but the heat generated by atmospheric friction would severely confuse the infra-red sensors, thus effectively limiting the speed which could be attained. Because of the time required for each rocket or projectile to reach its target, missiles would only be vulnerable if there was a rocket carrier virtually overhead. This would mean that an effective defence would have to launch an extravagant number of such carriers in order to compensate for the large numbers which would be out of range of their targets at any one time. Even at the current level of Soviet armaments, the cost of simply lifting such a fleet into orbit would be around $13 billion.[7]

Mid-course Interception

The second phase of the three-layer plan involves attempting to intercept the nuclear warheads released by the surviving boosters as they travel through space. This is regarded as the most difficult and uncertain phase of the whole operation because of the difficulty of finding and tracking the warheads in the 20–30 minutes between separation from their boosters and re-entry into the earth's atmosphere over their targets. Whereas the ascending boosters were made conspicuous by their bright rocket plumes, the warheads once in space would emit only feeble infra-red radiation. Detection of such targets would require cryogenically cooled sensors with a sensitivity many orders of magnitude greater than any currently attainable. In addition, for every real warhead deployed there would be many decoys designed to fox sensors and overload the battle-management computers. False warheads, metallic balloons, radar-reflecting chaff and infra-red reflecting aerosols would accompany the warheads on their journey, and it would be extremely hard to distinguish real warheads from decoys because in the vacuum of space all would travel at the same velocity. One possible method of dealing with this 'threat cloud' would be to attack every object regardless. This would be very expensive, and it would be hard to guarantee that any system could deal effectively with every type of decoy that the ingenuity of the offence could devise.

If it was decided to attack every single object in the threat cloud, a choice would then have to be made whether to use randomly homing devices or to use some form of central battle planning to assign specific targets to specific interceptors. If the former method was chosen, then even assuming a 100-per-cent hit rate the redundancy ratio for the defending weapons would be enormous. It has been calculated that for a 99.9-per-cent kill ratio against 10,000 objects in mid space some 70,000 devices would be needed. If the threat cloud contained 100,000 objects, which is quite possible, then the number rises to 700,000.[8]

Terminal Defence

The third stage of SDI involves intercepting warheads as they re-enter the atmosphere over their targets. At this stage in their flight the warheads again become distinguishable from the chaff, balloons and decoys which accompany them as the atmosphere sweeps them away. This appears to be technically a more straightforward problem than delivering knockout blows to boosters rising from Russian missile silos. However, ballistic-missile re-entry vehicles re-enter the atmosphere at enormous speeds, making tracking and targeting, in the short time remaining for interception, very problematical. If a terminal defence was installed the opposition could fairly easily adopt additional penetration aids such as making re-entry vehicles which manoeuvre unpredictably on sensing an attack. All the same, a terminal defence could plausibly be constructed which would defend one or two missile silo fields. A warhead must be delivered with great precision in order to destroy a hardened missile silo, and interceptor missiles would have a great deal longer to find their targets than they would over a soft target such as a city.

But supposing that a reasonably foolproof area defence system could be built? It would then have to deal with a hypothetical attack of unknown proportions and architecture. An enemy might choose to concentrate the whole, or a large part of its missile force on a few selected targets with the intention of overwhelming such a defence; indeed a perfect defence would have to be able to deal with the launch of the whole Russian ICBM arsenal against a single unspecified target. Since ABM interceptor rockets must travel at speeds limited by atmospheric friction (i.e. speeds in the range of those of the re-entry vehicles themselves) they would have a severely limited range, making massive redundancy inevitable. It has been estimated that even if the formidable technical problems could be overcome, in order to be certain of handling surviving re-entry vehicles from an attack by 1,400 ballistic missiles the United States would have to build a fleet of 280,000 interceptors.[9]

COUNTER-MEASURES

The foregoing considerations give an idea of the massive scale of the operation proposed by President Reagan. However, all these calculations have been made using assumptions most favourable to the defence, i.e. no growth in the size of the Soviet arsenal, no development of counter-measures, and so on. But the bursting apart of the ABM and SALT treaties which 'Star Wars' implies is unlikely to produce such a situation. Once the treaties are abrogated there will be no incentive for either side to restrain production of nuclear weapons and indeed the Russians have recently made it clear that they will counter the American SDI programme by a nuclear build-up aimed at penetrating such defences rather than by a parallel space-defence programme of their own.[10]

Many possible counter-measures to the various elements so far discussed are known. Indeed the properties of the boost-phase intercept system which we have been discussing are based upon the fact that current ICBM missile inventories were designed without such interception in mind. Booster rockets follow a 'minimum-energy trajectory', which is to say that their flight is planned in such a way that they can carry the maximum number of warheads and decoys using the minimum amount of rocket fuel. Hence the SS-18 takes a leisurely five minutes to boost itself to the altitude where it launches its weapons, thus giving a whole five minutes for decision, aiming, and destruction of its booster. However, there is no reason why a booster has to burn for this long, and the most effective counter-measure against all forms of boost-phase interception is therefore to shorten the boost time so that the telltale infra-red-emitting rocket plume is extinguished at an earlier stage. This would be remarkably effective since, as we have seen, most of the types of interception available, and in particular the otherwise promising X-ray laser, are ineffective below a certain level in the atmosphere. The rocket manufacturers McDonnell Douglas testified before the US Congress that for a modest increase in cost of about 10 per cent a rocket booster could be produced which would complete its boost phase in as little as forty seconds. This would completely nullify many of the systems for boost-phase destruction which we have outlined above.

Suppose, though, for the sake of argument, that a super-high-energy chemical laser could be produced which could reach deeply enough into the atmosphere, react quickly enough and aim accurately enough, to strike at the ascending boosters during this first forty seconds of flight time. A variety of inexpensive counter-measures would then be available: for example, the boosters could be protected against the effects of the lasers. Possible measures include coating the whole booster with a material that burns off the skin of the vehicle, releasing heat as it does so. (This material is currently used to protect space vehicles against the heat generated during re-entry into the atmosphere.) The boosters could also be spun in such a way that an attacking laser beam would have to spend three times as long playing on the booster in order to deliver the same amount of heat to a given area on the booster's skin. The combined effect of these two simple counter-measures would be to force a tenfold increase in the number of laser stations required in orbit. Other more elaborate counter-measures could also be taken at this stage. These include confusion of the infra-red sensors which aim the laser beam and confusion of the laser radar with a large number of bright corner reflectors. One more elaborate method of attacking space stations in orbit would be to send X-ray lasers through the atmosphere to attack them. A laser beam which is very bright at its source is able to force its way through the atmosphere by a phenomenon known as 'bleaching', which means that an X-ray laser fired from within the atmosphere would have a greater range than one fired from space.

In the other layers of the SDI system the advantage would also remain with the offence. During the short period of the warheads' journey through space the defence would be confronted with a cloud of decoys of unknown design and capabilities. Some might contain nuclear material to confuse active sensors like neutron probes.[11] Others might contain warheads linked to other heavy weights in such a way as to confuse attacking missiles as to their centre of gravity. Infra-red sensors and radars could be blinded by exploding a few nuclear devices in the upper atmosphere, causing a massive and persistent glow at a great many crucial wavelengths. Other counter-measures in this phase include spoofing the mechanisms which confirm that a target has been hit, perhaps by throwing out fragments or causing the target to divide into several parts.

Terminal-phase interception allows the introduction of yet other counter-measures. Again decoys can be used, in this case more elaborate and expensive ones which simulate the weight and appearance of an actual nuclear warhead; decoys could emit ionized plumes, thus mimicking the envelope of hot gas surrounding a warhead; active decoys can be designed which, although small, are able to detect the pulse from the ABM radars and reply with an echo similar in profile to that produced by a real warhead.[12] A cruder but no less threatening counter-measure would be to resort to the use of extremely large warheads (say in the fifty megaton range) against centres of population. Such a warhead can cause massive damage even if exploded at high altitude, and could be 'salvage fused', i.e. fused to explode upon detection of an intercept.

Besides the tactical counter-measures outlined above, various strategic counter-measures would be available to an attacker facing an SDI-type defensive force. Kinetic-energy weapons in low orbits would be more efficient if their orbits could be arranged so as to pass over two or more ICBM sites, thereby allowing a smaller number of battle stations to be used to cover each missile-launching site. Conversely, however, such battle stations could be made less efficient by clustering ICBMs at fewer and more densely packed sites. Attack patterns could be chosen to exploit the particular weaknesses of the defensive technology chosen. For instance, chemical-laser battle stations and their associated command and control systems would have the maximum difficulty in dealing with a massive simultaneous launch which would require them to deal with a large number of targets in succession. Multi-barrelled X-ray-laser devices would suffer from a converse problem because in order to stop even a small launch of one or two missiles the weapon would have to destroy itself; such battle stations could be forced to 'commit suicide' if they were directly attacked.

ASAT – THE WAR OVER THE WORLD

Anti-satellite warfare (ASAT) is a particularly worrying prospect, both because of the negative effect which it is likely to have on the peaceful use of outer space, and because of the threat to the surveillance satellites which both superpowers currently rely on for early warning of possible attacks and verification of the provisions of existing treaties. Besides the obvious threat to peace from intentional destruction of vital reconnaissance and communications capacity during a crisis situation, litter from previous satellite launches, ASAT experiments and testing of the radar-reflecting properties of metal needles launched into orbit, etc., have greatly increased the risk of accidental damage both to surveillance and communications satellites and to manned space missions such as the projected American space station.[13] Two unexpected satellite failures have already been attributed to collisions with such space 'junk'. The unexplained failure of a crucial early-warning satellite during a time of international tension could easily be interpreted as the act of a hostile power, with highly destabilizing consequences.

ASAT has a special place in the 'Star Wars' inventory since the technology involved in satellite interception is undergoing active testing both in the United States and in the Soviet Union. Early versions of ASAT envisaged the explosion of nuclear warheads in the vicinity of satellites in order to destroy them from a distance. The United States installed a battery of nuclear-tipped ASAT missiles at Johnston Island in the Pacific, but these were dismantled in 1975, partly because it was realized that the detonation of nuclear warheads in space would have a counter-productive effect on the American communications and control network. Recent advances in computerized guidance systems have stimulated a new round of research into systems involving non-nuclear devices. Russian tests have involved the destruction of satellites in orbit by manoeuvring 'space mines' (i.e. other satellites containing high explosives) into proximity with them. Although crude, the Russian ASAT system has scored some successes. It is slow, however, since the interceptors can only be launched when their targets are in a favourable orbit. A more sophisticated American system involves the release of a miniature guided homing vehicle from a high-flying aircraft. This device has now been successfully tested. Although neither of these systems constitutes anything like a fully developed ASAT system at present, the American system is potentially more threatening, since it could be used to launch a coordinated attack on the low-orbiting Russian satellites whereas the Russian ASAT device does not seem likely to pose a threat to the US satellites in the foreseeable future.

ASAT research has threatening implications for the development of the arms race in space. Both sides are aware that the ABM Treaty does not forbid the testing of ASAT weapons *per se*, so long as it can be claimed that they have no ABM capability. Only the use of such weapons is forbidden. There is evidence that weapons researchers may use this loophole in an attempt to develop secretly a machine that could later be transferred to an ABM role. George Keyworth himself has stated that ASAT tests are '. . . important to test the technology to destroy missiles'.[14] ASAT devices would also play a large part in the counter-deployment to any orbiting SDI system. A situation might arise where, in order to protect interceptor satellites in specific orbits, the US or the USSR might have to declare 'total exclusion zones' in particular bands of earth orbit. Any space vehicle passing through these zones without prior clearance would be subject to instant destruction by satellite warships poised to defend the fleet.

Amongst weapons which are being proposed for an ASAT role are the usual panoply of laser and particle-beam weapons. It seems likely that these would be a great deal more effective in the vacuum of space than they would be against rockets rising through the earth's atmosphere. Satellites tend to be 'soft' targets. If they are involved in reconnaissance or data processing they contain sensitive sensors and electronic circuits which can be easily blinded or confused. Additionally, satellites can be tracked and targeted very easily since they travel for long periods of time in predictable orbits. This makes the prospects of building a space-based ABM system even more remote, since it would be virtually impossible to defend against the contingency of a massive attack from space itself. Besides counterattack with lasers and beam weapons, satellites are extremely vulnerable to destruction by hard flying objects, abrasion by sand or dust, etc. A swarm of rubbish released into an orbit opposing the orbit of a satellite would strike the satellite with a speed of ten miles per second, and at this speed a one-ounce pellet can penetrate six inches of hard steel.[15]

KEEPING IT ALL TOGETHER – COMMAND AND CONTROL

We have so far concentrated on individual technical aspects of an SDI system. As we have seen, these individual problems are large and very far from being solved in the present state of our knowledge. However, the problem of welding all these elements into a functional and effective whole is a problem which dwarfs the individual problems entirely.

C^3I (command, control, communications and intelligence) presents by far the largest challenge of any element in SDI and has been allotted the lion's share of the SDI development budget for the next five years, about 45 per cent of the whole.[16] C^3I was described by SDI Director James Abrahamson as the 'glue' that would hold the system together. Such a system would have to overcome many seemingly intractable problems in addition to the problems of communications and data-processing power outlined below. To function within the environment which would prevail during the outbreak of a nuclear war would mean finding a definitive solution to the problem of electromagnetic pulse (EMP). The seriousness of this phenomenon was first realized by scientists during atmospheric nuclear tests in the Pacific, when a nuclear airburst over Johnston Island extinguished street lights in Hawaii over eight hundred miles away. It was discovered that the explosion of nuclear weapons high in the atmosphere creates a powerful electromagnetic pulse which induces extremely high voltage gradients in electric and electronic components over a wide area of the earth's surface. Although certain limited and confined systems, such as ballistic-missile guidance gear, may now be hardened against EMP to the extent that they could be relied upon to function in an environment of nuclear attack, it is unlikely that the currently existing networks of computers and telecommunications would survive if a handful of nuclear weapons were airbursted with a view to disrupting them.[17]

A battle-management system for SDI would have to have a seemingly impossible set of characteristics. It would be required to be on alert at all times, to be capable of giving an error-free assessment of any attack pattern which might conceivably be devised and of responding to such an assessment with military force, almost certainly without time for human intervention. It would have to function despite attempts to disable it, and it would have to continue to function effectively over a period of time in an environment of nuclear bursts, jamming, spoofing and spurious electromagnetic radiation over a wide spectrum. Such a system would have to begin operation within a matter of seconds of detecting a first missile launch. Thereafter it would have to track many boosters, perhaps thousands of them, which could separate into tens of thousands of warheads and decoys. It would have to keep separate trajectories for all these objects. In the early stages of the attack the battle-management system would have to select targets for the lasers and kinetic-energy weapons in the correct order of precedence, and ensure that each target was assigned only one interceptor. It would have to follow up each strike in order to ensure that the target had been hit and destroyed. In order to achieve these stringent objectives, all space-based and ground-based elements of the battle-management system would need to be in continuous and uninterruptable contact with each other. The sensors and computers needed to run such a system would have to be of the order of a million to a hundred million times more efficient than those which exist today.[18] In addition to this, software of unimaginable complexity would be needed to operate the system. It would have to be coded in such a way that it was guaranteed to work on its first field trial without hitch. This is quite simply beyond our capabilities at present. All commercial and scientific software currently requires extensive field testing and adjustment before it can be released for use, and even then faults continue to be discovered throughout the operating life of the software. All software contains errors, but widely used commercial software tends eventually to reach a stage where the failures only occur under extremely unusual circumstances. No such process of trial and error would be possible for the software which would drive 'Star Wars'.

As an example of the hardware and software problems of battle-management systems it is instructive to look at the way in which NATO's military command and control network functions. This network in its current form derives from a major Pentagon report, produced in November 1961, on command and control problems. As a result of this report blast-proofed underground command posts were constructed at Omaha, Nebraska and Cheyenne Mountain, and a rotating system was established which ensures that at least one aircraft equipped to unleash the US strategic arsenal is airborne at any one time.

As a command and control system for a strategy based on pure deterrence, i.e. assurance of mutual destruction, the current system may be adequate. That is to say, even if a hostile power were able to disable both the President and his deputy and all the underground command posts in one strike, the nuclear machine would still be capable of retaliation, either controlled from the air by the 'looking-glass' flying command post or, in the last analysis, from US submarines. Current problems with the network of command and control make it doubtful, however, that the United States could actually respond to a nuclear strike in the controlled fashion that a 'Star Wars' defence would require. Successive Pentagon studies have pointed up weaknesses and flaws in the system. Vital early-warning satellites send their information via ground stations which use miles of unprotected underground cable and vulnerable commercial telephone links. Locations of vulnerable satellite control stations are freely published in congressional reports.[19]

The failures of the early-warning and command and control computers are notorious. Under current procedures all warnings of incoming missiles have to be verified by at least one other device, and read-outs from early-warning stations must be taken to confirm the attack warning received. When, in June 1980, a faulty circuit caused spurious warnings of what appeared to be an attack by submarine-launched ballistic missiles, it was this manual double-checking procedure, followed by a conference of the staff at NORAD, which led to the conclusion that the US was not under attack and that World War Three had not in fact begun.[20] In the intervening minutes, however, nuclear-armed bombers throughout the United States had been alerted and were taxi-ing for take-off. False alerts due to malfunction of electronic equipment are said to occur on average three times every year, along with additional false alarms caused by such diverse factors as radar reflections from the moon, flocks of geese, natural gas flares and other such unpredictable items.

Besides the instability of the early-warning system, the unreliability of the computers of WWMCCS, the grandly titled World-Wide Military Command and Control System, has become something of a national scandal in America. The system is based on thirty-five standard Honeywell computers which the Department of Defense bought as a job lot in the early seventies for reasons which nobody has so far been able to discover. The computers are intended for business applications which involve updating data files sequentially in batches, and are quite unsuitable for the interactive environment of a battle-management system. Even after spending over 100 per cent of the purchase price of the hardware on complicated software designed to overcome this inherent fault, the system was still so unreliable that in March 1976 a Defense Communications Agency official stated that 'the network crashes approximately every thirty-five minutes, while the longest time without a crash was approximately one hour'.[21] During a 1977 military exercise the WWMCCS computers were linked to the computers of the US Atlantic Command, European Command, Readiness Command, Tactical Air Command and the National Military Command Centre. During the exercise, communications between the systems were subject to an overall failure rate of 62 per cent.[22] In a similar exercise in November 1980, the WWMCCS computers failed completely for twelve hours.

SDI researchers hope to tackle the hardware problem by developing new generations of computers in which data transmission and switching is handled by light rays rather than electrons. European researchers, led by a team from the Heriot-Watt University in Edinburgh, hope to demonstrate the world's first optical computer in 1986. The road to perfect battle-management software has not been so easy to plot since it involves, as we have seen, consideration, along with the laws of dynamics and relativity, of Murphy's law, which states that if anything can go wrong, it will. Hopes for progress appear to depend upon breakthroughs in artificial-intelligence systems and nebulous techniques for 'computer simulation' of a ballistic-missile-defence situation. Not surprisingly, some of the most convincing expressions of scepticism have come from within the computing and artificial-intelligence community. In April 1985, both Stanford University and the California Institute of Technology announced their refusal to take part in classified research on an optical supercomputer. When George Bush visited London for a two-day stopover in June 1985 he was presented with a petition signed by seventy-eight top British computer scientists affirming their refusal to involve themselves in research for an SDI system which would be 'impossible to design, impossible to build and impossible to test'.[23]

Space is a shallow ocean – beyond the confines of the earth's orbit and our own solar system lie oceans of relativity too deep to cross.

Nevertheless, space is a reservoir of startling and fulfilling insights. The star map is probably one of the earliest man-made objects still in existence, yet our knowledge of the stars is still growing and flowering and amazing us with their diversity and wealth of paradox in a way that would have seemed utterly unbelievable to our ancestors.

In March 1986 the European space probe Giotto will encounter Halley's Comet. Protected by a fragile shield against bombardment by debris, it will attempt to manoeuvre to within a hundred kilometres of the comet's nucleus and to photograph its icy interior for the first time. In order to achieve such a close contact it will be reliant on information from two Russian Vega probes which will pass the comet more distantly just a few days earlier. It's not 'détente' or East–West cooperation that's at work here, but human beings who share a quest for knowledge about their own provenance and the provenance of the earth which supports us.

Science is the story of humankind's genius for curiosity, and as with all good stories there exists an adaptation for children. SDI with its particle beams and invulnerable fortresses is a children's version of science, written simply, with larger-than-life empires of good and evil and with a happy ending that nobody really believes. The tragedy is that this version of science now appears to be about to subsume the other, as though a degenerative shift were taking place in the centre of gravity of our collective consciousness. While we dream about reaching for the stars our own little bit of space is closing in on us and we are filling it up with expensive and useless junk. If the space-weapons race and the ASAT tests continue, it has been estimated that the dangers of accidental collision with spent satellites and pieces of shrapnel will make manned spaceflight unacceptably hazardous within a decade.[24]

Finally, we should point out that SDI offers no protection against cruise missiles, submarine-launched missiles, and a host of other technologies available to an opponent who wishes to overwhelm it. It is truly a closed system, existing only in the imaginations of those individuals and corporations who stand to gain, in their own estimation, from embarking on it. Dr Robert Bowman, of the Institute for Space and Security Studies, should know. During the 1970s he was in charge of the Defense Advanced Research Projects Agency, doing research into just such systems:

Every time we designed a dollar's worth of defence, we found it could be neutralized with a nickel's worth of offence ... to tell the American people that all they have to do is scrap the ABM Treaty and open their wallets and the government will make them safe from nuclear weapons is to foster a dangerous delusion.[25]

3 · Assessing the Soviet ABM Programme

John Pike

Public assessments of the Soviet–American strategic balance are too frequently coloured by perceptions of a present or impending 'gap' in American capabilities. The 'gap' is one of the standard arguments that is used in favour of an increased US effort on some type of weapons system. But in retrospect, these 'gaps' have proved to have a perverse reality. There was once indeed a bomber gap, and also a very real missile gap, and both were overwhelmingly in America's favour.

One increasingly popular justification for President Reagan's new strategic defence initiative is the assertion that there is now an 'ABM gap'. The 1985 edition of the US Defense Department Publication, *Soviet Military Power*, includes a description of the Soviets' strategic defence activities that runs on for over ten pages, in contrast to the five pages allotted this topic in the 1983 edition. The illustrations in the 1985 edition provide a remarkably detailed portrait of the Soviet ABM effort, and include information, derived from reconnaissance satellites, of a type that would previously have been regarded as unreleasable.

The status of the Soviet ABM programme is of legitimate concern for American strategic planners. American missile defence research is in many regards paced by the Soviet programme. One generally accepted rationale for the American BMD programme is to provide a hedge against Soviet break-out from the ABM Treaty, and to deter such a break-out by maintaining a technological edge. The American ABM programme also provides a basis for understanding and assessing Soviet developments, and for designing counter-measures to possible Soviet defences.

There is indeed an 'ABM gap'. But like the gaps of previous years, the ABM gap is in America's favour. The United States continues to enjoy a significant lead over the Soviets in this field. This lead has been maintained for over a decade by a prudent programme of research, funded at a generally constant level. The state of the Soviet ABM programme does not offer any basis for a drastic acceleration of the

American ABM programme of the sort proposed by the Reagan administration.

ABM SYSTEMS – A FAMILY TREE

ABM systems may conveniently be divided into four generations, each of increasing capability, which are now at varying stages of maturity in both countries. The United States has essentially abandoned the first- and second-generation systems, is in the process of perfecting the third generation and is making some progress on the fourth generation. In contrast, the Soviets are only just now making the transition from the first to the second generation, and face very real obstacles to further immediate progress.

First-generation ABMs are single-layer systems such as the American Nike-Zeus and the Soviet Tallinn and Galosh systems; they use a variety of mechanically steered radars to guide a long-range rocket interceptor armed with a high-yield nuclear warhead in an attempt to destroy incoming warheads just before they re-enter the atmosphere. These systems can be readily defeated by relatively simple counter-measures, and are ineffective against attacks of any significant size or sophistication.

Second-generation ABMs are two-layer systems such as the American Nike-X, Sentinel, Safeguard, Site Defense, and Low Altitude Defense system, and the new Soviet ABM-X-3 system. These systems utilize more capable phased-array radars, and both long-range rockets, such as the Spartan, for interceptions outside the atmosphere, and high-acceleration short-range rockets, such as the Sprint, to intercept incoming targets during re-entry. Although this generation is clearly much more capable than its predecessor, it also has major shortcomings. The radars of these systems are very expensive, they are vulnerable to direct attack and are also subject to blinding by the explosions of their own interceptors.

Third-generation ABMs are multiple-layer systems based on technology that has been under active development in the United States for over a decade. There is no direct evidence of Soviet work in this area, and indeed such systems require technologies, such as computers, that are probably beyond the state of the art in the Soviet Union today. In the place of radars, these systems have mobile air-based and space-based infra-red sensors, such as the Airborne Optical System. Non-nuclear 'hit-to-kill' kinetic-energy interceptors, such as the Homing Overlay Experiment, can intercept targets both in and above the atmosphere. Third-generation ABMs constitute a significant advance over their predecessors. The mobile sensor platforms of these systems are much less vulnerable to direct attack than fixed radars, and kinetic-energy weapons avoid the self-blinding effects of their nuclear predecessors.

Fourth-generation ABMs are multiple-layer systems that include directed-energy weapons of various sorts. The principal attraction of these systems is their potential for intercepting missiles during their boost phase, when they are relatively vulnerable and before they can deploy multiple warheads and decoys. Thus these systems have stimulated considerable discussion in recent years, but this attention is in some sense premature. Although both the US and USSR have active programmes for the development of some of the techniques required for such systems, both countries are clearly many years, if not decades, away from perfecting these devices.

CURRENT SOVIET ABM ACTIVITIES

The Soviets are now in the process of making the transition from their early first-generation ABMs, the Tallinn and Galosh, to a new second-generation system, the ABM-X-3. By contrast, the United States made this transition about two decades ago.

The SA-5 'Tallinn' System

In 1963 the Griffon interceptor was paraded in Red Square, and characterized as an ABM interceptor. Construction of this system was first detected in the early 1960s near the Estonian capital, Tallinn. An additional thirty sites were detected under construction near Leningrad. However this construction soon ceased. A highly modified version of the Griffon, the Gammon, was subsequently developed. Today more than a thousand anti-aircraft Gammon launchers are operational around about a hundred Soviet cities.

When this system was first noticed in the West, there was considerable debate over its mission and capabilities. Although the deployed air-defence system does have some minimal ABM capability, there is now general agreement that it is essentially restricted to an air-defence role. In general, its performance seems to be similar to that of the American Nike-Hercules air-defence missile.

The ABM-1 Galosh Moscow System

The ABM-1 Galosh missile was first seen in a parade in Red Square in 1964, and Soviet commentators characterized it as an ABM interceptor. It has never been seen in public except in its launch container. In the late 1960s construction started on eight launch sites for this system in the vicinity of Moscow, with four of these sites actually becoming operational. In 1980 two of these sites were de-activated, in anticipation of subsequent upgrades. Each site has sixteen launchers with associated radars and battle-management computers.

On the whole the performance of the Galosh would seem to be similar to that of the American Nike-Zeus. The use of mechanically steered radars and high-yield nuclear warheads substantially limits the effectiveness of this system, which could be easily saturated by even a small attack.

The ABM-X-2 System

This system, incorporating various improvements over the ABM-1, was under development in the early 1970s. This system was probably conducted in parallel with the more capable ABM-X-3 system as a hedge against the failure of that development effort. Work apparently halted in the late 1970s. Essentially no information on this system is available in the open literature.

The ABM-X-3 System

Since the mid-1970s the Soviets have been pursuing the development of a more advanced follow-on to the Galosh system. This new system, the ABM-X-3, will probably become fully operational at Moscow by 1987. Five new launcher sites are under construction, and two Galosh sites are being converted for the new system. There is some dispute as to whether the ABM-X-3 is actually a new *system*, distinct from the ABM-1-B, or will simply incorporate several evolutionary improvements. In either case, the ABM-X-3 components are equivalent to American ABM technology of the early to mid-1960s, inferior even to the US Sentinel/Safeguard ABM system. The ABM-X-3 shares many of the technical limitations and vulnerabilities of the US Nike-Zeus (i.e., dependence on a limited number of mechanically steered radars for tracking and guidance).

The ABM-X-3 will incorporate several improvements over the Galosh. Existing mechanically steered radars will be replaced by somewhat more capable radars that incorporate some aspects of phased-array technology. And two types of interceptor missiles will be used, taking advantage of atmospheric bulk filtering to discriminate decoys from actual warheads. The interceptors will be deployed in underground silos to reduce their vulnerability to direct attack. Nonetheless, the ABM-X-3 will be at best the technological equivalent of the US Sentinal/Safeguard system of the 1960s.

The components of the ABM-X-3 include:

• The SH-4 long-range exo-atmospheric interceptor missile which is somewhat smaller than the massive Galosh and is probably a three-stage solid-fuel rocket with a range of 300–400 km. This interceptor may use a sub-megaton-yield neutron warhead to destroy incoming re-entry vehicles just above the atmosphere, or it may retain the high-yield warhead of its Galosh predecessor.

• The SH-8 short-range endo-atmospheric interceptor is probably a two-stage solid-fuel rocket with a range of less than 100 km and a low-yield nuclear warhead. It is generally similar in design and mission to the US Sprint missile, although its maximum acceleration is reportedly significantly lower.

Recent press reports indicate that in at least one test of the SH-8 short-range ABM interceptor, two interceptors were fired from a single launcher at an interval of two hours, although no reloading equipment was observed in the area. No other details on this incident have come to light. It is not entirely clear how this observation was made. Satellites would not provide continuous coverage of the area. Given the short battle time available to ABM systems, two hours does not seem to be particularly 'rapid'.

• The Flat Twin target track radar will replace Try Add radars at Moscow ABM sites to track incoming targets for interception by SH-4 and SH-8 interceptors. Flat Twin is a hybrid of conventional mechanically steered and phased-array radar technology, with a phased-array antenna that is mechanically pointed in the direction of the target. This suggests that, as with the previous all-mechanical Try Add radars, one Flat Twin radar will be required to track each target. This modular radar can be erected on a concrete apron at a prepared site in a matter of three to six months.

• The Pawn Shop missile track radar, which is housed in a van-sized container, will also be installed as part of the Moscow system. Like the Flat Twin radar, Pawn Shop is both transportable and modular in the sense that it can be disassembled, moved in component stages, and reassembled in a period of several weeks. This, however, assumes that some advanced preparation of the site upon which it is being re-located has occurred.

• The Pushkino large battle-management phased-array radar which is under construction near Moscow provides 360° coverage and will supplement Dog House and Cat House radars in supporting SH-4 long-range interceptors.

• The Pechora-type bi-static phased-array early-warning radar will supplement the Hen House radars. Deployment began in the late 1970s at seven sites: Pechora, Lyaki, Mishelevka, Olenegorsk, Sary Shagan, Kamchatka and Abalakova. The new Pechora-class radar near the Siberian village of Abalakova in the Krasnoyarsk region is situated hundreds of kilometres from the Soviet border, and is thus inconsistent with the 'at the periphery' requirement of the ABM Treaty. The coverage of this radar includes most of eastern Siberia, and is very difficult to reconcile with the 'oriented outward' requirement for early-warning radars. These inconsistencies have led the Reagan administration to raise this issue in the SALT Standing Consultative Commission. The Soviets have responded that the Abalakova radar is a space-track radar, and thus exempt from the limitations placed on early-warning radars. Although the Krasnoyarsk radar would not seem to add much to existing Soviet satellite-tracking capabilities, its location and capabilities may be suitable to support an advanced anti-satellite weapon system (similar to the new American system) which would engage and destroy target satellites while they were over the Soviet Union. While there may be both legal and technical merit to the Soviet argument, as a practical matter the radar is inconsistent with the intent and purposes of the Treaty (see pp. 87–8).

SOVIET AIR DEFENCE AND ABM

The Soviet Union maintains a large air-defence system, designed primarily to intercept and destroy enemy tactical aircraft before they can attack targets inside Soviet territory. This air-defence system includes over 1,000 sites and 12,000 launchers for the various types of interceptor surface-to-air missiles (SAM) the Soviets keep in their inventory. The performance characteristics of Soviet SAMs have been progressively upgraded over the years.

Clearly this is an expensive proposition. US intelligence-community estimates place the annual cost to the Soviets of buying new air-defence rockets, radars and aircraft in excess of $6 billion. This does not include operating and personnel expenses.

The assertions of some Reagan administration officials that the massive increase in the SDI budget is simply a response to Soviet strategic defence spending lumps together apples and oranges, aggregating Soviet air-defence costs with the budget for their BMD programme. Frequently overlooked is the fact that the United States is currently spending about $2 billion for strategic air defence (with significant future increases planned) in the face of a much smaller threat than is faced by the Soviets.

The technology required to intercept high-speed, high-altitude aircraft and cruise missiles is similar in some respects to that required to intercept ballistic missiles. Some in the US intelligence community have long been concerned with the possibility that Soviet air-defence missiles and radars could provide the base for a nationwide ballistic-missile defence system. This concern has increased recently because there are indications that the latest generation of Soviet SAMs, like their US counterparts, may be to some extent effective against tactical and theatre ballistic and cruise missiles, giving them an anti-tactical-missile capability.

However, it is possible to exaggerate the missile-defence capabilities of the Soviet air-defence forces. Most of the Soviet SAMs, such as the SA-1, SA-2 and SA-3, are armed with conventional high explosive warheads, and lack the performance required for an ABM mission. The SA-5, SA-10 and SA-12 do have some ABM potential, but this potential is rather limited.

It should also be recalled that the Soviets have not demonstrated overwhelming proficiency even in the less demanding task. Actual combat experience has indicated the need to fire between fifty and a hundred SAMs to down a single plane. With these ratios, the entire Soviet SAM force could be expected to intercept no more than a few dozen missile warheads.

But the task of intercepting a missile warhead is in many respects considerably more demanding than the task of intercepting a plane. The radar cross-section of a missile warhead is typically several orders of magnitude less than that of a plane. The warhead will also be accompanied by dozens or hundreds of decoys and fragments of the booster rocket, whereas the plane travels alone. The radars that are normally deployed with SAMs are clearly inadequate to deal with these demands, and would have to be supplemented with much more capable systems.

The velocity of a ballistic missile warhead on re-entry varies from about 3 km/sec. for shorter-range missiles or those with older, high-drag re-entry vehicles to about 7 km/sec. for intercontinental missiles with modern low-drag warheads. This is in contrast to the 1 km/sec. maximum velocity of a high-speed plane.

A SAM such as the SA-5 might be able to achieve a maximum velocity of about 1 km/sec., and a very high performance SAM such as the SA-12 might be able to achieve a velocity of 1.5 km/sec. In contrast, the Spartan, a long-range American ABM interceptor, had a maximum speed of about 3 km/sec.

The relatively low speeds of the Soviet SAMs severely constrain the area that the SAM could defend against ballistic missiles. The effects of atmospheric drag can be used to filter warheads from other objects at an altitude of between 40 and 60 km, depending on the sensitivity of the battle-management radar. At these altitudes, an ICBM warhead is about 150 km and 25 seconds from its target. Under these conditions, the SA-5, if it were guided by a very powerful radar, could intercept a slow-moving warhead (such as was used on US ICBMs in the early 1960s) at a range of several dozen kilometres. But the SA-12, guided by its present radar, would be hard-pressed to intercept a faster modern low-drag warhead at a range of more than a few kilometres. While the SA-5 might have provided for a limited defence of cities several decades ago, the SA-12 probably does not have that capability now.

The SA-5

The SA-5 Griffon was originally developed as part of the Tallinn system in the early 1960s, and was judged to have both an anti-aircraft and anti-missile capability. But the Soviets were apparently un-impressed with its ABM potential, as it has actually been deployed in the heavily modified Gammon version in an anti-aircraft role. The missile has a comparatively modest acceleration rate, and relies on its small wings for manoeuvrability. Both characteristics reduce its ABM potential. Furthermore, the mechanically steered radars used by the SA-5 are vulnerable to saturation by decoys.

During 1973 and 1974 the Soviets were observed using the radars associated with the SA-5 in conjunction with ballistic-missile tests, in possible violation of the ABM Treaty. When the issue was raised in the Standing Consultative Commission, the Soviets drew attention to the provision of the Treaty which permits use of radars for range instrumentation, and maintained that this was the purpose for which the SA-5 radars had been used. Within a few weeks after the issue was raised, the activity stopped, and has not been repeated.

In early 1985, after many years of negotiations in the Standing Consultative Commission, the Soviet Union agreed to further restrictions on its anti-aircraft radars. In the future, when ABM tests are conducted at the Sary Shagan test centre, all air-defence radars in the area will be turned off, unless there are Chinese or other potentially threatening foreign aircraft in the area.

The SA-10

The SA-10 is a new Soviet SAM that is roughly equivalent to the American Patriot, which is credited with a limited tactical ABM potential. When this system was first noticed, it aroused some concern over its ABM potential. More recently this system has been regarded as being primarily intended to counter very-low-altitude targets such as cruise missiles. Concern over ABM potential has been transferred to the SA-12.

The SA-12

The SA-12 is a new high-performance surface-to-air-missile system that the Soviets have been testing for several years. This truck-mounted system has been code-named 'Gladiator' by NATO. It is still undergoing tests, but is expected to become operational within the next year or two. The SA-12 is a hypersonic missile that is capable of executing very high-speed manoeuvres to engage targets at altitudes in excess of 100,000 feet. It is reported to have a range in excess of fifty miles, while the missile's truck-mounted radar is reported to have a range of over 150 miles. If, as is expected, the SA-12 were deployed with a nuclear warhead (like the SA-5, and unlike other Soviet anti-aircraft missiles), this system could have the capability to intercept some types of long-range ballistic missiles such as SLBMs.

If the SA-12 were to be deployed in conjunction with a more capable radar, it could approach the performance requirements for interception of longer-range missiles. But the limited acceleration and manoeuvrability of the SA-12 (compared to that of an ABM interceptor such as the American Sprint) would make such a defence very vulnerable to counter-measures such as heavy penetration decoys and even simple manoeuvring decoys.

Reportedly, on several occasions during 1983 and 1984, a version of the SA-12 was tested against a target vehicle that was based on an SS-12 tactical ballistic missile. This would be inconsistent with the ABM Treaty *only* if the SA-12 system were 'tested in an ABM mode', which is banned by Article VI(a) of the Treaty.

On 7 April 1972, the US SALT delegation made a unilateral statement on this issue that: '. . . we would consider a launcher, missile, or radar to be "tested in an ABM mode" if, for example . . . an interceptor missile is flight-tested against a target vehicle which has a flight trajectory with characteristics of a strategic ballistic missile . . .'

No definition of a 'flight trajectory with characteristics of a strategic ballistic missile' was agreed to in the ABM Treaty. Within the US government, the Department of Defense has in the past proposed demanding criteria for defining such a trajectory, i.e. if a target reached an altitude above 40 km and a velocity greater than 2–4 km/sec. Although a definite American position on these criteria was not reached, let alone one with the Soviets, it has been the Pentagon's position that if a SAM is tested against a target vehicle with such a trajectory, it should be considered as being 'tested in an ABM mode'.

While the SS-12 target reportedly did reach an altitude above 40 km and a velocity greater than 2 km/sec., it is difficult to conclude that a test against a target based on the SS-12 medium-range missile constitutes a test against a target 'with characteristics of a strategic ballistic missile', and is therefore inconsistent with the restrictions in Article VI(a).

Several senior US defence officials have also commented on the relation of the SA-12 to the ABM Treaty. Franklin Miller, Director of Strategic Forces Policy for the Department of Defense stated in 1984 testimony before the Senate Armed Services Committee that: 'The Soviet system SA-X-12 . . . is an air-defence system which has an anti-tactical-ballistic-missile capability. There is nothing in its development that contravenes the ABM Treaty because that treaty deals with strategic anti-ballistic missile systems.'

On 9 March 1983, in testimony before the House Armed Services Committee, T. K. Jones stated that '. . . the Soviets are developing that [the SA-12] to counter shorter-range ballistic missiles and the ABM Treaty was drafted so that it is a legal development and they could deploy it fully'.

FUTURE SOVIET ABM INITIATIVES

It is to be expected that the Soviets will continue their efforts to improve their ABM capabilities through research on more advanced third- and fourth-generation ABM technologies. But in many of the scientific and technical fields that are crucial for progress on these systems, the United States enjoys a clear technical lead over the Soviets, notably in the areas of advanced computers, infra-red sensors, and non-nuclear kinetic energy interceptors. Although the Soviets have a significant directed-energy programme, both countries are very far from fielding effective weapons of this sort.

Third-generation ABM Systems

The key components of effective third-generation BMD systems are highly capable battle-management computers and extremely sensitive and discriminating sensor systems. At present the United States holds a major lead in both of these areas. Indeed, the United States holds a commanding lead in virtually all of the major technologies associated with advanced ABM systems. Each year the Department of Defense publishes an assessment of comparative Soviet and American basic technological capabilities. Of the list of the twenty most important of these, thirteen are applicable to advanced ABM systems, including directed energy, computers, electro-optical sensors, signal processing and rocket propulsion. Of these thirteen, the Pentagon believes that the United States holds a lead in twelve areas, with the Soviets on par with the US only in the area of directed energy (and as the subsequent section will explain, Soviet parity even in this area is open to question).

In the field of advanced computers, capable of executing in excess of a hundred million instructions per second, interest is increasingly focusing on the use of computers to design both hardware and software; using fourth-generation computers to design fifth-generation computers. The Soviets are still struggling with third-generation computers.

Infra-red heat-seeking sensors offer major improvements over radars for boost-phase and mid-course interceptions. This is a field where the United States holds a significant lead over the Soviet Union. To date, the Soviets have not demonstrated a mastery of this challenging technology. Whereas the United States has routinely used infra-red sensors on early-warning satellites in high-altitude geostationary orbits, the Soviets have failed in their one attempt, in 1975, to emulate this technique. Furthermore, the Soviet infra-red guided anti-satellite system has failed in all six of its tests.

In the course of events, it should be expected that the Soviets will develop and test infra-red-guided kinetic-energy weapons. This programme will differ from the US programme in at least two respects. First, it will probably lag behind the American effort by a number of years. The first US flight test of the Homing Overlay Experiment (HOE) took place in June 1982, and the first successful test was not until June 1984. Weapons of the type demonstrated in the HOE programme will not be available for deployment by the US until the early 1990s. Similar Soviet tests are unlikely before the end of this decade.

Second, when these tests do come, they are likely to be much more numerous than their American counterparts. The entire Homing Overlay programme consisted of four test flights. These were preceded by a very intensive programme of tests in simulation facilities. Soviet deficiencies in simulation and computation will force them into a much more extensive and expensive series of flight tests than would be needed in the US.

Fourth-generation Directed-energy Systems

The Soviets have placed considerable emphasis on their directed-energy weapons programme, much to the alarm of the more easily excited members of the Western intelligence community. However, the most that can be said for the Soviet programme is that it is at approximately the same level of achievement as the US programme, and a more detailed look at their effort suggests that here, too, there is a perceptible American lead of as much as five years.

The Soviet laser programme is dispersed among a number of facilities, including the Sary Shagan ABM development facility in central Asia, where there are at least two large lasers. Additional laser development work is conducted at the nuclear-weapons test centre thirty-five miles south of Semipalatinsk, at Azgir in Kazakhstan, at the Dubna and Troitsk physics research facilities near Moscow, and at two or more lesser facilities. Particle-beam research is conducted at the Semipalatinsk nuclear-test facility.

There are significant differences between the two countries' programmes. The Soviet level of effort appears to have been greater than in the US, employing perhaps 10,000 personnel, several times as many as the approximately 3,000 in the US. This widely quoted estimate is based on the following methodology. Various open sources and technical collection means are used to establish the location of directed-energy research facilities. The buildings at these facilities are photographed by satellite, and an estimate is made of the total floor space in each building. Dividing the total floor space by the average floor space assumed to be used by each worker results in an estimate of the total number of people employed in the directed-energy weapon programme. Some analysts take this process one step further, and multiply this personnel total by an assumed annual wage and supporting costs to arrive at an estimate for the total budget of the Soviet programme.

The problems with this methodology are obvious; not the least of them is that it measures inputs, not outputs. There is a similar disparity in agriculture, with the Soviets devoting over a quarter of their national product to agriculture, while the US devotes less than 5 per cent, although no one complains of a 'grain gap'. Additionally, it is not always possible to separate Soviet research into areas such as inertial confinement fusion from work on directed-energy weapons.

Furthermore, Soviet research efforts are typically characterized by a productivity per unit of input that is about 40 per cent of that of their American counterparts. And in a cutting-edge technology, such as directed-energy research, this productivity is likely to be even lower. Whereas the American programme can count on a wide network of established commercial suppliers for basic components and spare parts, in Soviet research facilities most of these items must be made in the laboratory. Thus much of the floor space at Soviet labs is dedicated to workshops and craftsmen not catered for in American research facilities.

Additionally, American laboratories have access to vastly more powerful computer facilities than are to be found in the Soviet Union. American research is increasingly computer intensive. In contrast, lacking such computers, Soviet research is hardware and personnel intensive, which requires larger facilities to achieve equivalent results. The parity of results is illustrative of the much lower *per capita* productivity of Soviet science.

A recent Central Intelligence Agency report on the Soviet directed-energy programme offered additional insight into the status of their effort. In particular, the CIA compared the power levels achieved in the two countries using various types of lasers. Early American leads in gas-dynamic and electric-discharge lasers have been eclipsed in the past five years. This is largely a result of an American decision that these lasers would offer poor prospects as weapons, and that further development was unwarranted. In the more promising chemical lasers, the United States continues to hold a lead of at least five years. In general, the Soviets have not had much success in developing the lightweight, fuel-efficient lasers which seem to have the greatest potential for space-based applications.

Soviet persistence in devoting significant resources to less-than-promising technologies may reflect the reward structure in the Soviet economy as a whole, where fulfilment of the norms of the Five-Year Plan is at a premium. Under these conditions, it might be preferable to continue work on a well-understood technology, rather than risk failure on more novel devices, even though these might offer greater pay-off in the long run.

The Soviets have made a number of original contributions in directed-energy research, particularly in the field of particle beams. The Radio Frequency Quadrapole technique, which offers significant improvements in the performance of particle-beam weapons, was a Soviet development, reported in the open Soviet literature, and subsequently incorporated into the American weapons programme.

The Soviets also published the first detailed description in the open literature of the nuclear-pumped X-ray laser. But there is evidence that the Soviets have lagged behind the United States in the actual development of this technique. Soviet test results seem to be less promising by several orders of magnitude than those in the United States.

It is significant that many Soviet 'firsts' are in areas of basic science, where the Soviets are admittedly strong. The transition from theoretical principle to working weapon continues to be a major Soviet weakness. It is also significant that the areas of Soviet 'firsts' are those, such as particle beams, that show the least promise for deployment in the short term.

Over the years there have been a number of published reports that have suggested that the Soviets had achieved a substantial lead in directed-energy weapons. In retrospect, the reports have all been discredited. In the mid-1970s there developed a considerable controversy within the intelligence community over the function of a facility at Semipalatinsk, with some arguing that it was a nuclear-bomb-pumped particle-beam weapon of tremendous power. Subsequently, it has been determined that the device is a pulsed-iodine laser of rather modest military potential. Possible indications of Soviet laser attacks on US early-warning satellites were later attributed to large fires at Soviet gas wells. Reports of Soviet astronauts on the Salyut space station being advised to put on special goggles to protect their eyes from laser light may seem alarming at first glance, but seem much less sinister when it is recalled that low-powered lasers are routinely used by many countries to obtain precise tracking data on satellites.

One Soviet directed-energy innovation that has received considerable attention is the possibility in the future of an integrated on-orbit test of a space-based laser. Some analysts in the Defense Intelligence Agency have speculated that such a test could come any time between 1984 and 1990. There are several reasons for this speculation.

The US laser programme currently anticipates an analogous on-orbit demonstration in the 1993 time-frame. Given the rough parity between the Soviet and US programmes, and the observed tendency of the Soviets to field-test at an earlier stage than the US, the suggested timing is not implausible.

Additionally, the Soviets have been observed making preparations for a large space-launch vehicle, similar in size and capability to the American Saturn V moon rocket. Although various potential missions have been identified for this new launcher, including a manned trip to Mars and a large space station, it is difficult to place a great deal of credence in these explanations. However, a large space laser would clearly require a launch vehicle of this magnitude. At a minimum, the development of such a launcher must be regarded as an effort by the Soviets to keep their options open should a decision be made to proceed with the testing of a space laser.

Nonetheless, there is general agreement that the actual military significance of a possible Soviet on-orbit demonstration of a space laser would be rather difficult to identify. The initial prototype will certainly have fairly marginal capabilities. And the laser itself is the least challenging element of an integrated weapons system. The pointing and tracking sensors, and the battle-management command and control systems are the most critical elements of an effective space-weapon system, and these are areas of known Soviet deficiencies.

CONCLUSIONS

Despite strenuous efforts, the Soviets continue to trail the US by a wide margin. Soviet ABM systems under development and in deployment typically lag behind their American counterparts by at least a generation. The American equivalent of the deployed Galosh system is the Nike-Zeus, which was under development in the 1950s. And the new ABM-X-3 system is the technological equivalent of the American Sentinel/Safeguard system of the 1960s.

Assertions of a major Soviet lead in this field are highly disingenuous at best. One frequently hears the assertion that the Soviets are a decade ahead of the US. In fact, this is based on the Soviets' development of a large space booster that could be used to orbit space-based weapons, and the claim that the United States will not have a similar capability until the late 1990s. This ignores the fact that the US successfully used such a booster, the Saturn V, to send astronauts to the moon fifteen years ago.

Soviet design and procurement practices differ greatly from those in the US and often give the appearance of a lead that does not exist. Given the limitations of the Soviet scientific and engineering community the Soviets must invest several times the level of American personnel and facilities to achieve equivalent results. Developmental experiments that can be conducted in the laboratory or using computer simulation in the United States require actual field testing in the Soviet Union.

The Soviets tend to field militarily ineffective systems in order to gain operational and training experience. Whereas the low operation and personnel costs make this a viable proposition for the Soviet military, higher American costs render this sort of activity rather marginal. The real military significance of the Soviet activity is difficult to identify. In addition, the unique symbolic significance of Moscow, coupled with the reality of the nuclear threat to this region, combine to provide an incentive for a limited Soviet ABM deployment. Fortunately, the United States does not have similar incentives.

The Soviets have generally maintained a fairly good record of compliance with the ABM Treaty, indicative of a strong degree of commitment to it. Since the early 1970s, occasional Soviet activities have raised questions regarding their strict compliance with the terms of the ABM Treaty. Past compliance issues have included the possible testing of an air-defence-system (SA-5) radar in an ABM mode, failure to report the dismantling of excess ABM test launchers adequately, and the construction of an ABM test range on the Kamchatka peninsula. All of these issues were discussed in the Standing Consultative Commission and resolved to the satisfaction of both parties.

Despite the satisfactory resolution of these issues, the dynamic pace of the Soviet programme continues to give rise to questions concerning compliance with the Treaty. The most troubling of these is the new radar at Abalakova, near Krasnoyarsk, which is very difficult to reconcile with American interpretations of the Treaty. This issue is now under discussion in the SCC. Several other matters have received publicity, but have not been raised in the SCC. Given present assessments of the direction of the Soviet ABM programme, it is possible to anticipate that in the future several new compliance issues might arise. Whether or not these actually materialize will of course depend on specific Soviet actions.

Nonetheless, there is little evidence of a concerted effort on the part of the Soviets to break away from the ABM Treaty in the near future. The Soviets seem to have demonstrated the capability to deploy components of an ABM system rapidly. But the United States demonstrated the same capability over a decade ago.

Soviet incentives to break out from the ABM Treaty are rather difficult to identify. The systems that are available to them at the present time, and for the foreseeable future, are of only limited capabilities and marginal effectiveness. These would not seem to offer the prospect for a cost-effective investment for the defence of hardened military targets. And they hold virtually no promise for the defence of urban/industrial targets.

The United States has maintained an active programme for the development of penetration aids, and this programme was reaffirmed in President Reagan's National Security Decision Directive 91 of August 1983. At present, American strategic missiles, and in particular submarine-launched ballistic missiles, carry an extensive complement of penetration aids which would severely tax any prospective Soviet ABM system. The deployment by the Soviet Union of a significant ABM capability would require several years at a minimum. This would be more than enough to add any additional penetration aids that were thought to be needed to overcome the Soviet defence.

But wider political considerations might prompt the Soviets to disregard these objections, and to proceed with deployment. If the United States was perceived as making major strides toward perfecting third- or fourth-generation ABM systems that the Soviets were unable to match, they might feel impelled to actually deploy a less effective second-generation system. Such a Soviet system could be operational many years before the more advanced American system, and could rectify, though temporarily, the perceived imbalance in capabilities.

The ABM Treaty of 1972 is the foundation of all efforts to achieve limitations on offensive strategic weapons. At present neither side has the ability to defend itself effectively against an attack, nor does either country have such a defence in prospect. This is particularly true for the Soviet Union, which trails the United States by about a decade in the development of such systems. In the absence of severe provocation, Soviet incentives for abrogation of the treaty are difficult to identify. And despite the American technological edge, legitimate and compelling incentives for the United States to break the treaty seem equally elusive.

4 · The Effects of SDI on Disarmament

Rip Bulkeley

Nowhere has the Strategic Defence Initiative given rise to greater controversy than over its implications for nuclear disarmament. Its apostles call on us to share their hope that missiles will begin to be abandoned on all sides, once they are rendered 'impotent and obsolete' by Star Wars technology. President Reagan has declared:

> In the long-term, we have confidence that SDI will be a crucial means by which both the United States and the Soviet Union can safely agree to very deep reductions, and, eventually, even the elimination of ballistic missiles and the nuclear weapons they carry.[1]

Eminent critics reply:

> The argument that actual deployment of US defences – at a level short of perfection – would provide leverage to gain significant reductions in Soviet missile forces seems to fail on logic as well as on common sense.[2]

The President's men have a problem. On other days of the week they have been arguing that an alleged *Soviet* build-up in defensive as well as offensive forces has provoked, not a sudden American urge for 'deep reductions', but the massive current *increase* in US nuclear forces. It is not very clear why this offensive-build-up sauce, with which they have smothered but hopefully not yet cooked the Western goose, would not also be adopted by the Eastern gander on perceiving a parallel situation.

So another line about SDI and disarmament has also been provided. We are told that SDI will break neither the letter nor the spirit of any existing treaty for many years to come. If ever the time came for testing or deployment of new anti-missile systems which would go beyond what is now permitted, then and only then would consultations and negotiations be in order, first with America's allies and later with the Soviet Union:

> President Reagan has made clear that any future decision to deploy new defences against ballistic missiles would be a matter for negotiation.

This does not mean a Soviet veto over our defence programmes; rather our commitment to negotiation reflects a recognition that we should seek to move forward in a cooperative manner with the Soviet Union . . .

Of course, arms control would play an important part in such a transition [to a 'mix of offence and defence']. Properly structured cuts in offensive arms are not only worthwhile in their own right; they could also facilitate the move to a more defence-related posture.

Before negotiating such a cooperative transition with the Soviet Union, and throughout the transition period, we would consult fully with our allies.[3]

To sort out competing claims about the probable effect of SDI on the world's chances of nuclear disarmament, we need to take some fairly general bearings by which to navigate the murky waters of what governments and their servants refer to as 'arms control'.

THE TANGLED WEB OF ARMS CONTROL

Even those who invented arms control knew it was the third-best option. The best response to the devastation, moral as well as physical, caused by the dropping of the first atomic bombs would have been a natural turning towards and growth of a united or at least a federal world. Second-best would have been steady progress in large-scale disarmament negotiated between stubbornly sovereign states. After about fifteen years, when this no longer seemed possible, a new approach was substituted. If the political reality was that actual disarmament could not be achieved, perhaps the opposed powers could at least find ways to limit and channel the arms race, and so reduce the risk of nuclear war? This substitute for disarmament was euphemistically known as 'arms control'.

But arms control has proved a mess of contradictions. If both sides of the world arms race had common security interests, that should logically have led them to undertake cooperative disarmament and other joint arrangements. If they were not prepared or able to do this, and each sought protection in continued military competition, even within agreed limits, then what were they doing pretending to have security needs and interests in common?

The usual answer is that they were and still are bowing to world public opinion. That's us, reader. But don't flatter yourself. They only bow to public opinion in order to shackle it. Negotiators may proclaim their concern for 'peace' and 'disarmament'. But talks are actually conducted by the two opposing superpowers with an unceasing eye to the main power-political chance. Every negotiation becomes a bloodless battle for propaganda advantage in the global political struggle, above all over Europe, that cockpit of the Cold War. Every line of every treaty is haggled over to ensure it means no loss of mythical nuclear might. Every phrase is hedged about with silent, one-sided interpretations and with cold-blooded decisions about future weapons programmes which will allow the bypassing of restrictions nominally agreed to. As one expert has depressingly concluded:

> The arms-control agreements hitherto reached have not halted the arms race or reduced the military potential of states. In many cases, the weapons prohibited have had little, if any, military importance, and the outlawed activities have never seriously been contemplated as methods of war. Negotiations on measures which could make a significant impact on the arms situation in the world have stagnated for years.[4]

With arms control explained in this way, we are better equipped to understand the gaps and confusions in the treaties dealing with the arms race in space. (These will be described below.) It is instructive to compare these products of the arms-control process with international treaties and codes dealing with such matters as maritime insurance or the regulation of civilian air traffic. These fill page after page with detailed and comprehensive definitions and provisions, clearly intended by all concerned to take a firm grip on every imaginable situation. A typical arms-control agreement, by contrast, consists of two or three pages of terse and badly written paragraphs, whose object often seems to be to obscure, rather than to explain, exactly how they are meant to take effect. As we shall see, this is especially true of bilateral agreements – such as the crucial ABM Treaty – between the Soviet Union and the United States.

Another crippling feature of such treaties is that, by definition, neither party has any expert and authoritative outside forum to turn to if it feels the other has been cheating. But the two sides usually have conflicting aims and expectations, and the text of each agreement is crafted accordingly. Each party is therefore virtually bound to feel the other is breaking 'the rules' once they have retreated into their customary over-armed, mistrustful and irresponsible isolation to interpret the agreements in their own self-interested terms.

No arms-control treaty has a separate, purely legal life of its own.

Each is a marker, precariously attached to one aspect of the living and changing relationship between the superpowers. As that relationship blossoms or wilts, so does the treaty. But no matter how warm the political climate may from time to time become, most arms-control agreements are based on an essentially negative perception of their common interests by the two sides.

This explains, not just why the world's independent peace movements have been so critical of the failures of arms control, but also why they sometimes paradoxically seem to be defending it. For despite all the disappointments and betrayals, it is essentially an acknowledgement of the urgent common interest in abating, and even more in ending, the nuclear arms race. Cold War fanatics want to throw off even the token common sense of arms control; we, on the other hand, argue that the only thing worth preserving from the whole sorry shambles is the dim spark of constructive globalism which still survives.

Despite the resurgence of independent peace movements in the past decade, the militarists have had the best of it so far. For arms control to have achieved anything at all, however slight, it had to be sustained by continual new initiatives and agreements. But it is now twelve years since the United States last ratified a major nuclear-arms-control treaty with the Soviet Union, over space weapons or anything else. When we review the existing treaties dealing with arms control in space, we sometimes seem to be looking back at a bygone era, to a time when that small particle of humane rationality within the arms-control process had not yet been condemned as a treason against 'the free world'.

ARMS CONTROL IN SPACE

In the late 1950s, when the first intercontinental nuclear missiles (ICBMs) were imminent, and when it seemed likely that the Soviet Union would match or even surpass the technological efforts of the United States to build them, American politicians adopted an ideology of 'peace in the heavens' and called for a ban on the sending of weapons of mass destruction through 'outer space'. There were major problems with this approach. For one thing, there was no agreed definition of 'outer space'. (There is none to this day.) Also, the Soviet Union was aware of the all-out US drive for ICBMs at the time, and had little reason to expect that the generals of Strategic Air Command would be persuaded to renounce the new technology once it had become available. And indeed, not long before, the Eisenhower administration had browbeaten SAC out of its (job-protecting) obsession with manned bombers into taking nuclear missiles seriously as the *essential* strategic weapon of the future. In short, the whole affair was a typical piece of 'arms control', and a fitting prelude to much more of the same.

The first arms-control agreement to impose a restriction on military use of space was the 1963 *Partial Test Ban Treaty* between the USA, USSR and Britain, later signed by over a hundred countries. The treaty bans 'any nuclear-weapon test explosion, or any other nuclear explosion', both from 'the atmosphere' and 'beyond its limits, including outer space' (thus avoiding the problem of determining the boundary between them). This treaty would clearly be broken by any realistic test programme for the development of Edward Teller's nuclear-bomb-powered 'X-ray laser' (p. 36).

Before long, outer space, still undefined, received its very own treaty, this time through the negotiating machinery of the United Nations. The 1967 *Outer Space Treaty* bans nuclear and all other 'mass-destruction' weapons from any form of stationing in outer space. It requires that all 'celestial bodies', including the moon, be used 'exclusively for peaceful purposes' and that no military bases, weapons tests or manoeuvres should occur on them. The value of this prohibition can best be appreciated by seeing that it is still resented in some influential quarters:

I don't rule out a military lunar base in the next fifty years.[5]

However, although the treaty requires all activities anywhere in space to conform to international law and to be conducted 'in the interest of maintaining international peace and security', it stops short of outlawing all military uses of space, particularly by satellites in orbit around the earth. Though some have tried to claim that the requirement for legality and peacefulness rules out *any* military uses of space, this was not its purpose, nor does the wording support such an interpretation. Had that been the intention of the parties, it could have been plainly stated in the treaty. It was not.

A third element of arms control in space was introduced in 1972 by the first *Strategic Arms Limitation Agreement*, SALT I, and re-affirmed in its ill-starred 1979 successor, SALT II, whose ratification was blocked in the American Congress but whose provisions have nevertheless been informally observed by both superpowers until the time of writing. These agreements ban any interference with the 'national technical means of verification' (NTM) of both sides. This effectively legitimizes the use of military spy satellites for early warning, photographic and electronic intelligence, and some forms of ocean surveillance. It makes *use* of anti-satellite weapons against such targets illegal. But it does not cover attacks on military weather, geodetic and navigation satellites, or against civilian satellites. (The latter probably have some nebulous legal protection under the Outer Space Treaty.) Since US navigation satellites (Navstar) are now also platforms for nuclear-explosion detection devices (NUDETS), which may be deemed a sort of early-warning system, they may be protected by this provision.

ARMS CONTROL OR 'SPACE CONTROL'?

Until 1980 it had been accepted for about twenty years by the world's most powerful governments that:

The elimination of nuclear and conventional armaments must be so phased that at no stage will any country or group of countries gain a significant military advantage.[6]

Although in negotiations the superpowers might struggle more or less transparently for military advantages, in fact they were more interested in pursuing political gains. The Reagan administration is different; it has openly avowed its determination to turn away from an arms-control approach to security in pursuit of decisive strategic superiority, the nuclear philosopher's stone. Reagan was not merely playing to the patriotic gallery during his 1980 campaign when he said:

Since when has it been wrong for America to be first in military strength? How is military superiority dangerous?[7]

Two years later his Defense Secretary is said to have commented, after revelations about the goals for strategic superiority set by his top-secret defence guidance document, that anyone in his job who was not planning to prevail in a nuclear war would deserve to be impeached.

This desire for decisive US strategic supremacy has been loosely associated with an interest in the possible military uses of space for over thirty years. The accession to power of a right-wing administration made for an abrupt decline in the regard paid to the niceties of arms control in space. This can best be shown by allowing leading members, supporters and advisers of the administration to speak for themselves:

PRESIDENT REAGAN

No nation that placed its faith in parchment or paper while at the same time it gave up its protective hardware ever lasted long enough to write many pages in history . . . The argument, if there is any, will be over which weapons, and not whether we should forsake weaponry for treaties and agreements.[8]

Arms-control arrangements for space are desirable if they contribute to *our* overall deterrence posture and reduce the risk of conflict, not as ends in themselves [emphasis added].

DEFENSE SECRETARY WEINBERGER

I have never been a proponent of the ABM Treaty.[10]

I am not one of those who feels that an active and effective ballistic-missile defence system is destabilizing. The sooner we can get to it, the better I like it . . . Obviously if we were able to destroy incoming missiles effectively, I don't think it's destabilizing. I think it would be extremely comforting.[11]

I can't imagine a more destabilizing factor for the world than if the Soviets should acquire a thoroughly reliable defence against these missiles before we do.[12]

ASSISTANT DEFENSE SECRETARY PERLE

I am sorry to say that [the ABM Treaty] does not expire. That is one of its many defects . . . I would hope that were we to conclude that the only way we could defend our own strategic forces was by deploying defence, we would not hesitate to renegotiate the treaty and failing Soviet acquiescence . . . I would hope we would abrogate the treaty.[13]

PRESIDENTIAL SCIENCE ADVISER KEYWORTH

We do not want any negotiations for a couple of years or more, in order to get our [SDI] programmes going full blast.[14]

ARMS TALKS AMBASSADOR NITZE

There could be serious arms-control negotiations, but only after we have built up our forces. [When would that be?] In about ten years.[15]

ACDA DIRECTOR ADELMAN

My policy would be to do it [arms control] for political reasons. I think it's a sham.[16]

AIR FORCE SECRETARY ALDRIDGE

The harsh fact is that space may soon become the last, best place for the US to establish and maintain combat superiority.[17]

SENATOR GOLDWATER

Space is just another place where wars will be fought and I think America's technological superiority and electrical genius ought to be allowed to go forward.[18]

SENATOR WALLOP

Any nation which deployed two dozen ... first-generation chemical-laser [battle] stations would command the portals of space against the rockets of any other nation.[19]

SENATOR WILSON

As the Italian historian Francesco Guicciardini wrote almost five hundred years ago, 'You are only truly safe from the man you suspect when he cannot harm you even if he wants to. Security founded on the will and discretion of another is false.'[20]

HERITAGE LOBBYIST GENERAL GRAHAM

The multi-layered ballistic missile [defence] approach could filter out up to 90 per cent of attacking re-entry vehicles with their nuclear warheads, moving the US and Soviet Union away from mutual assured destruction to assured survivability *for the US* [emphasis added].[21]

Under such leadership one feels little surprise at the adoption in 1983 by the US Air Force of a space plan which calls for the preparation of weapons for use in space, for 'space control' and for downwards 'force application' of anti-missile systems and of general-purpose 'space-to-earth weapons'. The plan defines USAF missions as follows:

To prevail in theatre conflict, the Air Force must seize the initiative and quickly achieve both air and space superiority ...

Space superiority is required to ensure that our space-based assets are available to support theatre forces. Superiority in space will require a robust force structure and the capability to destroy hostile space systems.[22]

What such policies will actually be taken to imply, by those Americans who work at the sharp end of the arms race, need not be left to our imagination. First speaks an 'idealist', a young PhD student and former Boy Scout, who 'when he first came to [Lawrence] Livermore [Laboratory] ... had reservations about working on weapons, but eventually put them aside' to work all out for Uncle Sam, on the supercomputers essential for what he has learned to call 'weapons of life':

> We can try to negotiate treaties and things like that. But one thing I can do personally, without having to wait for arms control, is to develop the technology to eliminate them myself, to eliminate offensive nuclear weapons.[23]

Next a 'realist', a senior USAF weapons development planner, enthusing over current plans for a shuttle-like Trans-Atmospheric Vehicle, or 'space fighter':

> Wouldn't it be great if the Soviet Union suddenly found itself faced with the United States Air Force having a machine that could operate on its own, totally free from counteraction, capable of rapidly delivering weapons anywhere on the globe?[24]

We need scarcely comment ourselves on whether such a one-sided superiority, extreme enough to realize the Reagan vision of abandoning 'treaties and agreements', and difficult 'things like that', for the 'weaponry' of 'assured survival', would really be all that 'great'. Nor need we cite the predictable views of Soviet leaders. General Brent Scowcroft, who chaired the prestigious bipartisan presidential commission on strategic forces during President Reagan's first term, has said it all for us:

> ... one of the first casualties [of SDI], if we're not careful ... is likely to be arms control.[25]

In recent years, this conflict between arms control and the goals and practices of US space-weapons development has been clearest and most public in the squabbles between the Reagan administration and Congress over the current US anti-satellite-weapon (ASAT) programme.

THE ASAT PROBLEM

Anti-satellite-weapon programmes threaten to block disarmament in two ways. First, with the growing importance of non-weapon military assets in space, they pose the danger of a sudden acceleration of the technological arms race into an area which, as we have seen, is not yet covered by prohibitions or restrictions in any treaty. (The protection extended to spy satellites in the SALT agreements covers only the *use* of anti-satellite weapons against them, not the development of such weapons or their deployment in space.) Thus competition might escalate rapidly between systems for destroying satellites and very similar 'defensive' ones for destroying their anti-satellite cousins. Second, as analysts from all sides of the 'Star Wars' debate have pointed out:

ASAT is a much simpler technical problem than ABM defences that operate above the atmosphere . . . since the targets are softer, fewer, predictable both in their position and time, easier to discriminate, not easily replaced, and have communication and control links from earth that can be attacked . . .

The significance of ASAT for strategic defence lies in the threat it poses against the space platforms of the ABM, in particular against the warning, [target] acquisition and battle-management sensors. On the other hand, the significance of the Strategic Defence Initiative for ASAT is that it will spur technical developments that, inevitably, will be threatening to the critical communication and early-warning satellite links on which a ballistic missile defence will rely. This presents an unavoidable dilemma: ASAT threatens ABM, but ABM developments contribute to ASAT.[26]

Thus Dr Keyworth, Reagan's scientific adviser, has proposed as an early goal for SDI's laser-weapons programme the demonstration of a device 'powerful enough to act as an anti-satellite weapon' rather than of an anti-missile device.[27]

The anti-satellite system currently at an advanced stage of development in the United States is a clear case of the technology overlap between anti-missile and anti-satellite weapon systems. Its homing infra-red-guidance technology was originally developed for an ongoing anti-missile programme, the Homing Overlay Experiment, in which it was successfully demonstrated under artificially favourable conditions in the summer of 1984. For this reason a leading authority on arms control in space has stated:

. . . it is no use banning one of these [categories of] systems and letting the other go ahead. If there were only a ban on ASAT systems, the result would probably be that the technologies which were being developed for ASAT purposes would acquire a new label: we would be told that they were being developed for anti-ballistic-missile purposes. It follows that any action against the development or deployment of anti-satellite systems should be accompanied by equivalent action against anti-ballistic-missile systems.[28]

And vice versa, of course.

Neither before nor after the launching of SDI was the first Reagan administration ready to acknowledge this problem probably because it did not share its critics' approval of the arms control with which anti-satellite development interferes. Only in its final months, under steady pressure from a Congress itself strongly influenced by the Freeze movement, did the administration make a few reluctant, cosmetic and ineffective moves towards an ASAT treaty.

The story is too long to tell in full.[29] Talks between the Soviet Union and the United States about a possible ASAT treaty had been abruptly terminated by the latter after the Soviet invasion of Afghanistan in December 1979. With the Reagan team still holding its first defence review, and patently lacking any policy for arms control, the USSR sought to revive the issue by going through the United Nations, where in August 1981 it presented a draft treaty, 'On the Prohibition of the Stationing of Weapons of Any Kind in Outer Space'. Though represented as supplementing the Outer Space Treaty's earlier limitation to 'weapons of mass destruction' only, the text was inadequate as an ASAT ban, since it would have permitted the existing or planned anti-satellite weapons of both sides, which are stationed on earth rather than in space. It also contained a loophole, making attack on a space object legitimate if the attacker merely suspected that it carried a weapon in contravention of the treaty. The loophole was all the wider because the parties were not obliged to consult or to agree on such a crucial question, and because the term 'weapon' was left undefined.

By September 1982, however, concern was mounting in Congress at the lack of progress in this area of arms control. The Senate Foreign Relations Committee held special hearings, at which the Senators' anxiety was sharply increased by what they heard of administration thinking. Amongst other witnesses, the then Director of the Arms Control and Disarmament Agency, Eugene Rostow, explained that US reluctance to seek an agreement that would halt development of its own anti-satellite weapon derived not simply from anxieties about verification or about the existing ASATs of the Soviet Union (see p. 42), but also from an absolute, offensive military requirement for the means of 'countering the space components of threats to US forces' and 'the threat to our national security from advances in Soviet space programmes'.[30]

Dissatisfied with the administration's evident preference for exclusively military solutions to security problems in space, the Senate responded in July 1983 by passing an amendment to the defence budget. There would be no money for full-dress anti-satellite tests in space until the President could assure Congress, not just that such tests were necessary for US national security, but also that his administration was actually negotiating with the Soviet Union, 'in good faith', for an ASAT ban or limitation. The President was also required to produce a full report, by 31 March 1984, on his policy for anti-satellite arms control.

Meanwhile, the Soviet Union announced an indefinite moratorium on sending anti-satellite weapons into space, for as long as 'other countries, including the USA, will refrain from stationing in outer space anti-satellite weapons of any type'. The terms seemed carefully framed to permit at least preliminary testing of the American ASAT. This was followed a day later by a new Soviet draft treaty, with improved and far more comprehensive wording, which would prohibit all weapons in space and all weapons for attacks on space objects, whether from space or anywhere else. A major concession in the new proposal was a clause stipulating that signatories would scrap all existing ASATs, which would have been mainly applicable to the Soviet Union. The clause that would have prevented use of the American space shuttle for *any* military purposes was almost certainly included for bargaining purposes.[31]

The Reagan administration, however, remained inflexible. Instead of responding with positive counter-proposals, it launched an intensive domestic propaganda campaign to convince both legislators and public that the Soviet Union had been cheating on the ABM Treaty and other agreements, and that the military requirements for a US ASAT were imperative. In view of the more or less clean bill of health that had been authoritatively given to Soviet treaty compliance in previous years, the first of these two propositions was bound to prove an uphill task:

A special inter-agency commission was appointed by President Carter to investigate allegations of Soviet non-compliance made by opponents of SALT II. On the commission were representatives from the Joint Chiefs of Staff, the State Department, the CIA, the Arms Control and Disarmament Agency, and the National Security Council. This prestigious group found no evidence of Soviet cheating. The US Commissioner overseeing Soviet treaty compliance at the time stated: 'The commission has never yet had to deal with a case of real or apparent clear and substantial [Soviet] non-compliance with an existing agreement.'[32]

We shall return to the administration's claims about Soviet non-compliance shortly.

Not surprisingly, the President's March 1984 report on ASAT policy was negative. The congressional instruction that it should 'include specific steps the administration contemplates undertaking, within the context of US–Soviet negotiations, to seek a verifiable agreement with the Soviet Union to ban or strictly limit existing and future ASAT systems' was backhandedly observed by reporting that specifically no such steps had proved to be possible.

At about the same time a secret briefing to the Senate on Soviet ASATs alleged that there were as many as four types of anti-satellite weapon already actually in use against US spy satellites, using such techniques as blinding laser illumination and electro-magnetic radar jamming.[33] It seemed to be assumed without question that such inter-ference, if real, amounted to using 'weapons' in the full sense of the term. But such an interpretation appears doubtful in international law. The briefing succeeded in taking some of the heat off Reagan in election year. The congressional restriction on testing was reworded in broadly permissive terms. And the administration claimed to be working on a proposal for partial limitations, to be offered to the Soviet Union 'within a month'. As one unnamed official explained:

What's happening is it's an election year and the administration is losing its nerve. Having just concluded that this is an unpromising area for arms control, that decision may be in the process of being reversed.[34]

But when on 19 June 1984 the Soviet Union proposed a start to bilateral negotiations on 'preventing the militarization of space', the administration's nerve was not so far gone as simply to accept. National Security Adviser Robert McFarlane replied four days later accepting the idea in principle, but suggesting the preliminary discussions might also cover the intermediate-range and strategic-arms-control questions, which had been suspended by the Soviet walk-out in Geneva at the end of 1983. This linkage between space weapons and other arms-control issues proved temporarily 'unacceptable' to the Soviet government, despite its being a longstanding Soviet position. The talks proposed for Vienna in September 1984 never took place. Negotiations eventually resumed in March 1985, in a three-part package quite similar to what the Russians had found 'unacceptable' before Reagan's re-election.

But Moscow's determination to achieve American concessions in respect of SDI, and Washington's declaration that its Star Wars programmes are not negotiable, seem to make early progress with an ASAT ban, or on any other issue, rather unlikely:

> In hindsight, the early part of the 1980s will most probably be viewed as a fundamental watershed in the militarization of space. During this period the chance for a significant anti-satellite arms-control agreement was lost – possibly for ever.[35]

THE ABM TREATY

A MAD Idea

The 1972 *Anti-Ballistic Missile Treaty* between the USA and the USSR, amended in 1974, restricts anti-missile defences to a hundred fixed land-based interceptor missiles at a single specified site in each party's national territory. It tacitly permits laboratory research into anti-missile weapons that would not be fixed and land-based, but forbids their development to prototype or field-testing levels.

We have seen elsewhere that the treaty's restrictions were adhered to by both sides, though in different ways. That was because they had managed to agree, not merely on the main provisions of the treaty but also on the strategic philosophy of its Preamble:

> Considering that effective measures to limit anti-ballistic-missile systems would be a substantial factor in curbing the race in strategic offensive arms and would lead to a decrease in the risk of outbreak of war involving nuclear arms . . .

This is of course none other than our old unlovely acquaintance MAD, dressed up in diplomatic pinstripes. US politicians and ambassadors spent five hard years persuading their Soviet counterparts that strategic defences were potentially destabilizing because they would threaten the security supposedly derived from confidence in one's ability to retaliate even if the other side attacked first. Or, as McNamara remarked to Kosygin at a summit in 1967, about the Soviet ABM system then being deployed:

> You are trying to deprive us of our nuclear deterrent. And we will not let that happen.[36]

Sixteen years later, General Secretary Andropov, in the role of Echo, made reply:

The intention to secure itself the possibility of destroying, with the help of the ABM defences, the corresponding strategic systems of the other side, that is of rendering it unable of dealing a retaliatory strike, is a bid to disarm the Soviet Union in the face of the US nuclear threat.[37]

A 'survivable retaliatory capability' had been, and remains, the core of the whole Western theory of 'nuclear deterrence'. To abandon it and start an all-out ABM race would mean undoing all those years of reassuring everyone about the peace-keeping role of nuclear weapons. After all, if the threat of massive retaliation was enough to guarantee the nuclear peace, you didn't *need* ABMs. On the other hand, if you did need them, but they were declared to be technically impossible, that meant you had neither the guaranteed peace of 'deterrence', nor any protection from nuclear annihilation on that fearful day when the inadequacies of deterrence were found out.

Ever since the treaty was signed, experts have explained it was only made possible by an acceptance on both sides that effective large-scale anti-missile defences were simply not technologically available, even had the political decision been taken to pursue them. Thus, since the advent of arsenals of unstoppable nuclear missiles during the 1960s, the theory of nuclear 'deterrence' has laboured to extract some dregs of rhetorical virtue out of the grim facts of mutual vulnerability. And perhaps the ABM Treaty did little more.

Another of its features, the implicit toleration for continued research, was motivated by rather similar thinking. Since laboratory work could not be monitored reliably with spy satellites or any other 'national technical means', there was little point in attempting to restrict it. At the same time there was almost certainly an awareness on both sides that senior military officers would not have accepted any such restraint, verifiable or not.

Most strategists agree that anti-missile defences strong enough to cause instability – that is, to make it harder to stop crises developing into nuclear wars – can never be built using only ground-based interceptor missiles, together with their radars and control systems, all at fixed locations inside the national territory of either superpower. Nor are deployments of such 'traditional' ABMs, whether or not they carry nuclear warheads, at all hard to monitor from space. Mobile and space-based or space-using anti-missile weapons would be required for any truly 'strategic' defence, weapons able to intercept most enemy missiles in the first few minutes of their flight. To see how 'well' the treaty has worked, therefore, and whether it can go on doing so in the light of SDI and other current developments, we have to discuss the restraints it tried to place on the development of the potentially more effective forms of ballistic-missile defence (BMD).

Small Print

In line with MAD strategic philosophy, in Article I the parties agree not to deploy anti-ballistic-missile systems (ABMs) for a national, or regional, territorial defence, nor to provide 'a base' for such a deployment.

In Article II they define an ABM system as 'a system to counter strategic ballistic missiles or their elements in flight trajectory', and illustrate this by referring to current systems 'consisting of . . . ABM interceptor missiles . . . ABM launchers . . . ABM radars . . .'

Article III, revised by a Protocol agreed in 1974, permits one ABM deployment site, for fixed land-based missiles only. There may be no more than a hundred of these, together with two large phased-array ABM-guidance radars (PARs) and up to eighteen smaller ones inside the designated area.

ABM testing is limited to mutually agreed test ranges by Article IV, with no more than fifteen launchers on them.

In Article V the two parties undertake not to develop, test or deploy ABM systems or components which are mobile land-based, or sea-, air- or space-based, nor ABM launchers capable of multiple launches or rapid reload. The term 'based' is not explained.

By Article VI the parties bind themselves not to give ABM capabilities to non-ABM systems, nor to test such systems 'in an ABM mode'. Each agrees that 'radars for early warning of strategic ballistic attack' (not the ABM radars of Article III) shall be located 'along the periphery of its national territory and oriented outward'.

Article VII permits replacement and modernization of ABM systems or components, subject to the other treaty provisions.

Articles VIII and IX provide for the dismantling of any excess ABM systems and components, beyond the treaty limits, and forbid any transfer of ABM systems or components to other states.

In the remaining articles, the 'national technical means' (NTM) clause of SALT I is repeated, and provision is made for a permanent body, the Standing Consultative Commission (SCC), to promote the treaty's implementation and serve as a joint forum to handle all future issues concerning the treaty. Detailed procedures for reviewing, amending or unilaterally abrogating the treaty are laid down. Article XV declares the treaty to be of unlimited duration.

Some of the more obvious 'ambiguities, loopholes, and escape hatches'[38] in the treaty's main text are as follows: the terms 'element' and 'component' are used throughout without explanation; in Article II, the *example* of current systems risks being interpreted as part of the *definition* – this would make a nonsense of the treaty's broad intent, but that has not stopped some people trying it; Articles II and V between them do not say clearly whether ABM missiles with multiple warheads are banned; Articles II and VI do not define the concept of 'testing in an ABM mode'; Article V does not define 'based', which clearly means something different than the sense in which a bomber squadron has its 'base', not in the air, but somewhere on the ground.

Even Smaller

In a list of 'Agreed Statements' appended to the treaty proper, an attempt was made to improve matters. The most important by far is Agreed Statement D:

> In order to insure fulfilment of the obligation not to deploy ABM systems and their components except as provided in Article III ... the Parties agree that in the event ABM systems based on other physical principles and including components capable of substituting for ABM interceptor missiles, ABM launchers, or ABM radars are created in the future, specific limitations on such systems and their components would be subject to discussion ... and agreement ...

Since development and testing of all mobile-based ABMs and components is flatly forbidden already, by Article V, Statement D seems intended to cope with novel but *fixed land-based* systems, such as ground-based anti-missile lasers. Provided they *are* unambiguously of the fixed land-based type, the Statement appears in some sense to license their 'creation', but to register little more than a vague intention to talk about it when it happens. The wording is atrocious. Do such new devices have to be capable of substituting entirely for the old variety, or are they relevant as soon as they do so in part, as infra-red detectors have been doing for 'ABM radars' for many years, without any apparent agreement between the parties? (There may of course be a secret one.) Does the statement mean there should be no deployment of such new ABM devices unless there has been discussion, or unless there has been discussion and agreement? Or does making limitations 'subject to discussion' mean that pending discussion there are no deployment limitations?

Throughout the treaty and related documents there is never any mention of that essential preliminary to weapons development, research. It is generally accepted that restrictions on what goes on in laboratories would be meaningless, because, for practical purposes, they would be unverifiable. But if laboratory research is permitted and most subsequent development is not, the definition of where one ends and the other begins is crucial. Without such a definition, as US Congress members well understood at the time, the adversary's development of novel ABMs might proceed surreptitiously to a level just short of deployment, thus laying the basis for a rapid, strategically confounding 'break-out' from the treaty regime. On 18 July 1972, Ambassador Gerard Smith, US chief SALT negotiator, made this authoritative submission to the Senate Armed Services Committee:

> The obligation not to develop such systems, devices or warheads would be applicable only to that stage of development which follows laboratory development and testing. The prohibitions on development contained in the ABM Treaty would start at that part of the development process where field testing is initiated on either a prototype or a bread-board model. It was understood by both sides that the prohibition on development applies to activities involved after a component moves from the laboratory development and testing stage to the field testing stage, wherever performed.[39]

It is worth letting Smith explain the treaty-makers' thinking further:

> I do not think that's a loophole [Statement D]. You ought to look at Article I, where the parties agree not to deploy ABM systems . . . That is the heart of the treaty. It was agreed that, yes, you could do research and development on so-called exotic systems . . . but we recognized that space-based systems were especially dangerous because that is moving toward a nationwide defence system, and, therefore, we put them under more specific constraints in Article V, so you can't move to development. For [a fixed] land-based [system], however, you could move to development.

[On 'other physical principles':] The only fair interpretation is that any exotic system is banned. If it is developed and if it is not space-based, then before it is deployed both sides would have to agree that was permitted and that would be an amendment to the treaty.[40]

This interpretation stood uncontested for several years. Take, for example, the Arms Control and Disarmament Agency's annual report from early 1978:

Thus PBWs [particle-beam weapons] used for BMD which are fixed land-based could be developed and tested but not deployed without amendment of the ABM Treaty, and the development, testing and deployment of such systems which are other than fixed land-based is prohibited by Article V of the treaty.[41]

Ten years after Ambassador Smith's clarification, however, things had changed. As the commander of the then US Army Ballistic Missile Defense Organization, Major-General Tate, told the House Armed Services Committee on 24 February 1982:

We were limited in the scope of the R & D that we were allowed to carry out, part of it by congressional decree, from 1974 to 1980. For example, we were not allowed to prototype during those years. That restriction has been removed. We are now moving out and demonstrating the kind of hardware that is required if we are going to be able to reach an initial operating capability any time in the near term.[42]

That General Tate had not misunderstood his government's policy was to be dramatically revealed a few months later by Defense Secretary Weinberger himself, the day after Reagan's 'Star Wars' speech, when he declared:

. . . the Treaty goes only to block deployment.[43]

Pot and Kettle

The Reagan administration has published no less than three sets of 'findings' of Soviet non-compliance with arms control treaties in the past two years. Try as they might, the reports are studded with quali-fications such as 'potential breach', 'insufficient' or 'ambiguous' evidence, and Soviet actions which 'suggest' this, or are 'almost certainly' the other. Some sections deal with treaties not yet legally in force, thanks to American refusal to ratify them. One of the firmest accusations, of illegal transfer and use of Soviet chemical weapons in Afghanistan, Laos and Kampuchea, has been strongly called in question by independent bee-experts. On examining the 'yellow rain' dust in question, they determined it was simply bee faeces, regularly deposited in clouds by honeybees on mass 'defecation flights'.[44] Disregarding bullshit about bee shit, however, US claims of Soviet breaches of the ABM Treaty must be examined.

One charge is that Soviet actions 'suggest' they 'may be preparing' a national territorial defence, in breach of Article I.[45] This does not deserve separate consideration, since it depends on the force of the other claims. Another claim, that the Russians may be developing illegal mobile ABM components, is advanced so tentatively that, partly for the sake of brevity, we shall not discuss it. Two important issues in Soviet ABM activity remain.

The first concerns allegedly concurrent testing of ABM and SAM (air defence) components. There is general recognition by experts that technological advances are creating a 'grey area', with new anti-aircraft missiles slowly acquiring a level of capability, *on both sides*, which makes them partly effective against certain missiles as well. It is important to remember, however, that the ABM Treaty limits only systems for countering long-range strategic missiles. John Pike has examined the charge that Soviet air-defence and anti-tactical (ATM) capabilities could be upgraded to ABM functions in Chapter 3.

The second, in fact the only serious Soviet ABM issue raised in these reports is that of the large phased-array radar under construction at Abalakova, near Krasnoyarsk, in central Siberia (p. 55). The Russians say it is for tracking objects in space. The Americans say it is for ballistic missile warning. The argument will only be settled finally when construction is finished in two or three years, and the thing is switched on. Its character can then be read from the nature of its signals.

One authoritative assessment of the Abalakova radar, with impeccable Western credentials, has been a study by the British Cabinet's Joint Intelligence Committee. This viewed Soviet explanations as to its intended function as 'plausible', and considered that, while the Russians have 'a case to answer', the charge that the radar was designed for ABM missile guidance was 'unlikely' to be true. The contents of this highly secret report were passed to Washington, where someone leaked them to the press. They have not, of course, been presented to the British public, whose taxes paid for the exercise.[46]

If the Abalakova radar is for early warning of missile attack, then, as John Pike has shown, its location will be in breach of the treaty. The site is so far from the Soviet north-east coast (towards which the installation faces) that it might seem to be a poor choice for such a role. But the 'ballistic missiles' of the treaty's language include the submarine-launched variety. Interior siting for a large radar enables a wider ocean area to be watched than would a coastal location 'along the periphery'. The problem is that the treaty does not cater for systems intended to give early warning of an attack spearheaded by submarine-launched missiles – in the view of today's nuclear war planners, the most likely opening move.

Another drawback is that the treaty puts no restrictions on PARs for space-tracking and intelligence purposes (NTMs), but modern radars are increasingly capable of many different functions. Thus the USA has replied to Soviet criticism of its 'Cobra Dane' radar in the Aleutians that it is for both those functions and for early warning as well! Two large new PARs now under construction in the United States are set some way back from the coast, though not to the same extent as that at Abalakova, and this has been explicitly justified by reference to their role against SLBMs.

More doubtful are new American radar deployments overseas, in Canada, Greenland and also at Fylingdales in Britain. The treaty appears to forbid deployment of new early-warning radars in third countries, and that was the interpretation of it accepted by the Senate at the time.[47] The Reagan administration claims its radar deployments are permitted under the treaty's modernization clause in Article VII. But that refers only to radars which are components of actual ABM systems, not to the early-warning radars, which are clearly distinguished from them in the treaty.

On the radars issue, then, neither side can show the world a clean sheet. Even if Abalakova is for early warning, it seems to be part of a mutual pattern of treaty-bending. US overseas radar deployments abuse the treaty rather more, and are not matched by comparable Soviet infringements.

The Treaty's Over?

The whole radars argument is utterly trivial, however, when placed beside the implications for the treaty of SDI.

First, as we explained above, a treaty is more than a list of agreed measures. The ABM Treaty, in particular, embodied a declaration that defensive limitations were essential both for 'stable deterrence' and for any chance of progress in reducing offensive stockpiles. The Reagan administration denounces the failure of the arms-control process to deliver on the second of these two goals, and claims to have found a better way to arms reductions, by massive offensive increases plus SDI. This amounts in practice to a unilateral renunciation of at least the Preamble of the treaty. But if that is rejected, then so too are key phrases in the main text, about taking care to 'assure [the treaty's] viability and effectiveness', and so on. Even if neither side formally abrogates it for another decade or more, it is doubtful whether it can continue effectively in force under such circumstances.

Secondly, the Reagan administration is telling the Soviet Union and everyone else that all research and development in the SDI will be on the treaty side of the 'no field testing' line, but also that before Reagan leaves office in January 1989:

... we're going to be able to demonstrate technology that convinces the Soviets that we can – if we choose – develop a weapon to shoot down their entire ICBM fleet as it tries to enter space ... In this case we wouldn't be demonstrating a weapon, just a technique.[48]

What Dr Keyworth, the President's science adviser, is predicting here is a perfect, boost-phase-only defence, which in three years from now will have all its aiming, tracking, firing and battle-management technologies achieved to the level of convincing the Russians that no counter-measures, not even ones the Americans might not have thought of, would be any use. But this devastating demonstration will be achieved without building or field-testing the forbidden 'bread-board' models or prototypes of mobile anti-missile weapons, and without running any tests of the system as a whole, even if they are possible. Some technique!

Dr Keyworth must have received some very bad news from his weapons scientists in the next fortnight. Either that, or the change of audience from hawkish American Security Council on 4 June 1985 to pro-deterrence traditionalists at the European Atlantic Group in London on 17 June made him suddenly see things in a different light:

... achieving perfect defences [is] an unnecessarily stringent requirement. The President's ultimate goal of impotence and obsolescence for nuclear weapons isn't based on the need for such perfection ...

... boost-phase strategic defences ... create ... a *symbolic* dome over the East that prevents ballistic missiles from getting out ... [It may be] a *leaky* dome ... [but] it's more than effective enough as a deterrent against a first strike ... [Emphases added.]

... there will be nothing sudden about SDI.[49]

Development of anti-missile defences to the level hoped for by Dr Keyworth would not merely destroy the ABM Treaty, however, it would bring the whole arms-control edifice down in ruins, leaving nothing but a suicidal arms race in its place. In questions to the SDI's Director, General Abrahamson, Senator Nunn put his finger firmly on the spot:

Can you conceive of the Soviet Union developing a defensive system and as they develop it over the next ten years, we would reduce our offensive capability? ... You would come in and say to President Reagan, 'Mr President ... they can shoot down so many of our missiles that I recommend we decrease our offensive effort' ... I can't conceive of it.

The Senator's hapless victim was reduced to prayer:

I don't think anything in this country is technically impossible. We have a nation that can indeed produce miracles.[50]

But it would take more than patriotic bluster to refute the Senator's point, for the good reason that we scarcely need to guess what future Soviet reaction may be to the Reagan mix of anti-missile defences and a massive offensive build-up. Well before the speech which launched a thousand share-issues, the evidence of Reagan's longing for a space-based nuclear strategic supremacy was plain enough for Russian analysts to read. Four years later, the first stage of the Soviet Union's 'future' reaction to SDI is already with us, in the form of massive deployments of new strategic and medium-range missiles like the SS-24, SS-25, SS-N-23, SS-22 and SS-23, and the continued steady build-up of their SS-20 and cruise-missile forces. So far, the SDI seems to be doing for arms control what Prohibition did for teetotalism.

Nor does the Soviet response seem likely to be confined to building more offensive missiles, protecting them with better passive counter-measures, and planning for their possible use in ways most likely to fool or overwhelm the defences. Some suggestion can be detected in recent Soviet pronouncements to the effect that they will have to go down the route of 'active counter-measures', or space weapons, as well.

If the Americans militarize space against our country, we will have no option but to counter their move . . . With our kind of technological know-how we are capable of countering anything that the other side is capable of putting up.[51]

Counter-measures against the SBAMS [Space-Based Anti-Missile System] can be divided into two main groups: active and passive. The former include various ground [sea], air or space-based weapons using either missiles or lasers . . . The vulnerability of SBAMS adds to its destabilizing nature.[52]

What such language portends for arms control in space does not depend on whether it comes as a genuine response to SDI or is using SDI to excuse things the Soviet Union was already doing or preparing. Either way, this strategic policy and its Western look-alike suggest between them that for all its superficially humanitarian pretensions SDI can only aggravate the arms race.

Furthermore, a recent Greenpeace study argues convincingly that any transfer to another country of nuclear Star Wars weapons like the X-ray laser, or of their technology, for joint research and development, would be a major breach by the United States of Article I of the Non-Proliferation Treaty (NPT).[53] It would thus undermine still further one of the few multilateral arms-control agreements still more or less in place.

Pessimism about the likely effect of the SDI on disarmament prospects is no monopoly of those who criticize it, like ourselves, from within the world's non-aligned anti-nuclear peace movements. It has been widely voiced in Europe by some of NATO's staunchest supporters, such as Britain's Foreign Secretary:

I do attach importance to convincing the Soviet Union that we in the West are indeed serious in our aim of maintaining strategic stability at significantly lower levels of nuclear weapons. We do not want to give the impression that we have something else in mind. We are serious about arms control . . .

As the new negotiations . . . get under way, a key question for all our futures will be the extent to which reductions in offensive forces prove possible, and the impact this will have upon the incentive to develop defences . . .

Complete protection is not available for any country . . .[54]

Or, as the historian of nuclear strategy, Professor Lawrence Freedman, who does not have to speak in diplomatic language, has expressed it:

If the President really wants to eliminate offensive nuclear weapons from the face of the earth, why not propose just that to the Soviet Union? . . . If it is desired to limit the damage to the United States should deterrence fail, and reduce the risk of nuclear winter, then at the very least propose reductions to small stockpiles.[55]

5 · Folly's Comet

E. P. Thompson

For two years Star Wars orbited the globe in much the same form as it had been given at its first blast-off in President Reagan's speech of 23 March 1983. As it bleeped through political space its signals promised to the innocent observer a shield, or leakproof astrodome, which would bring to an end the immoral reign of MAD (mutual deterrence). We may call this Star Wars I.

By the end of 1984 Star Wars I was in difficulties. It had encountered the friction not only of the sceptical scientific community (especially in the United States) but also of America's European allies, who were not sure that they wanted MAD to end at all. In short, Star Wars I was re-entering the atmosphere of political realism. And at that moment a second satellite was sent aloft – Star Wars II – whose bleeps are signalling the exact opposite to those of its twin. It promised, not to abolish, but to 'enhance' deterrence. The resultant political and ideological confusions, the growth of specific military and industrial lobbies trying to turn SDI to their own ends, and the tensions within the NATO alliance, are the theme of this final chapter.

Star Wars I performed beautifully during Reagan's re-election campaign of 1984. It is difficult to credit the degree of planning which went into this operation, with the clear objective of confounding the American peace movement by stealing its lines. As early as 1982 a consultant to the Heritage Foundation's High Frontier project was writing that a space-defence project would give the US administration 'an opportunity to . . . fast-thaw the nuclear-freeze movement'. 'Armed with the detailed Heritage study . . . President Reagan would have the secret weapon needed to undercut the nuclear-freeze crusade.'[1] High Frontier's director, General Graham, commended his proposal as 'an effective counter to the nuclear-freeze movement around which the Left has been rallying and reviving the old McGovern coalition'.[2] The High Frontier study emphasized that the 'strategy of Assured Survival can be adopted and pursued without regard for further arms-control agreements with the Soviets':

Indeed, one of the salient advantages of High Frontier is that it provides security to the West quite independently of any trust or distrust of the leaders of the Soviet Union.

And, summing up the political character of the project:

> Adoption of the High Frontier concept could even convert or confuse some of the traditional opponents of defence efforts and technological innovations. It is harder to oppose non-nuclear defensive systems than nuclear offensive systems . . . It is hard to make environmentalist cases against space systems. Even those nay-sayers whose basic concern is disarmament will be hard pressed to make a case against High Frontier . . . [3]

This prescience was shown by High Frontier even before the President's speech. Early in 1984, during the run-up to the presidential re-election campaign, High Frontier received a detailed report from a consultant, John Bosma, on the political marketing of ballistic-missile defences. The objective of this project was to mobilize a popular lobby in order to ensure the start-up of BMD programmes during Reagan's second presidency, with sufficient momentum that it 'could not be turned off by a replacement or successor Democratic administration':

> This coalition could – and should – include members of the arms-control community; Democrats, liberals, and moderates of both parties; and foreign governments (especially Israel, Japan, France, Britain and Germany).

This 'in-house secret document' went on to set out each step of the strategy with care. 'Arguments and associated activism' should enable 'the US to move ahead forcefully and *unilaterally* with an urgent BMD programme', while at the same time there should be 'appropriate domestic and diplomatic activism' to represent the project as 'a *bilateral* effort – one with Soviet reciprocation and participation'. The project 'should unambiguously seek to recapture the term "arms control" and all of the idealistic images and language attached to this term' by emphasizing protection of civilians, 'just-war' conduct and the ways in which BMD is a practical way of realizing 'such highly lauded initiatives as a nuclear freeze, nuclear build-down and permanent disarmament'. 'A great deal of time' should be spent trying to get the 'vocal and outspoken' support of the governments of major US allies: 'there should be major efforts to develop an offshore constituency that is very sophisticated and whose voices will register in US debate'. One means proposed, to redirect domestic public debate, is to impute 'war crimes behaviours and intentions' to adherents of MAD-deterrence doctrine (and to supporters of the 1972 ABM Treaty) and to campaign for the USA to ratify the Protocols of the 1977 Geneva Convention:

> Innumerable opportunities for highly visible 'cause' activism could be opened up through a ratification drive for the 1977 Protocols, of the kind that naturally attract 'cause' activists of all persuasions; interest to Catholics also ... Such a ratification effort would permit the White House to look good in confronting powerful anti-BMD domestic critics.

As for the 'bilateral' effort, it is proposed that the United States should revive a long-forgotten 1962–3 Soviet proposal to the United Nations to reduce stocks of nuclear weapons alongside 'progressively thickened BMD and air-defence deployments'. This is recommended since 'it addresses "Eurostrategic" issues, which are big today', 'brings in US allies', and 'throws Soviet rhetoric back at Moscow'. Such unconventional 'shaking of the foundations' arguments are what are 'so badly needed in order to sell BMD'. They constitute –

> ... a radical approach that seeks to disarm BMD opponents either by stealing their language and cause [arms control], or by putting them into a tough political corner through their explicit or *de facto* advocacy of classical anti-population war crimes.

Mr Bosma then went on to consider how to get this lobby rolling, in such a way as to 'involve as many liberal or moderate constituencies as possible'. Perhaps a major political personality should be set up as lobby leader – Henry Kissinger was suggested. Or perhaps an umbrella group of allied interests? Mr Bosma favoured the second approach, which would 'concentrate on collecting lots of names'. This approach could 'tap the "urgency" element of the freeze movement [which] paradoxically represents the best mass constituency for an early IOC [Initial Operating Capability] BMD system – but only if an unorthodox and radical approach to selling BMD to peace groups is undertaken'.

Mr Bosma's High Frontier strategy paper ended by listing the 'target audience' to be enlisted in this lobby. High Frontier and other New Right groups should hide their sponsorship behind 'centrist' groups, 'neo-liberals and moderates', and should 'play freely on high-road ethical themes (by far the best mobilizational approach)'. The lobby should extend from its original supporters in Congress, the aerospace industry, the Heritage Foundation, the Hoover and Hudson Institutes, *Commentary* magazine and *Reader's Digest*, the *Wall Street Journal* and the (Moony-owned) *Washington Times*, veterans and pro-civil-defence groups, Ed Teller and selected members of the US laser community, and Republican Party strategists, to suggested soft targets among neutral or peace-movement opinion.

The sole objective of this High Frontier exercise (we must remember) was to get an initial operating capability of ballistic-missile defences off the ground during Reagan's second term and give SDI an unstoppable momentum. The cynicism of this well-funded salesmanship is such as to bring into question the integrity of all appearances. A movement to outlaw means of genocide (and to ratify the Geneva Protocols) is offered as a ploy to confound 'Soviet rhetoric' and to turn the tables on advocates of arms control. The peace movement is to be turned against itself. In the marketing of bad faith, the proponents of arguments about human destiny wear masks, and the zealous advocates of 'defence against missiles' (not only in the USA but also in Europe) may have a secret retainer from the US aerospace industry. The sales executives for the latest models of death rays now carry in their briefcases, along with their blueprints, volumes of Clausewitz, Gandhi and Tolstoy. Marketing of extermination is now a function of philosophy and ideology, and the means of war must be packaged as the means of peace.

Of course, this was only Mr Bosma's 'in-house' document. The Heritage Foundation was embarrassed by the leak and – even though it was circulated on Heritage paper – has disclaimed it.[4] Yet its own contribution to the 1984 election campaign was a volume, *Mandate for Leadership II*, which advocated US abrogation of arms-control treaties and the same takeover of the goodwill of the peace movement. The book came with an endorsement on the back cover from President Reagan: 'one of the people it's been most useful to and used by is me'.[5] The only real difference between the High Frontier lobby of General Graham and the Teller-plus-'kitchen cabinet' group around Reagan (pp. 18–19) is that the former are urging immediate 'off the shelf' deployments of BMD components (and support this with public lobbying) whereas the latter are closer to the seat of power and more involved in long-term development. General Graham could say with justice that High Frontier 'went public in March 1982 and by March 1983 we had the President of the United States saying this is the way to go'.[6]

They are still going much the same way today and promoting Star Wars I from the same ideological brief. In a fund-raising letter Citizens for a High Frontier state:

> This plan would make all of us safe from nuclear missile attack! If you fear nuclear weapons (and who doesn't?) you'll be relieved to know that this system uses no nuclear devices of any kind.

SDI is marketed as 'nuclear-free', just as American milk substitutes advertise themselves to the cholesterol-obsessed as 'strictly no milk content'. (For this reason the true ideologists have played down the Livermore X-ray laser, which could involve stationing nuclear devices in space.) And, following much the same lines, President Reagan told the National Space Club in March 1985:

> The Strategic Defence Initiative . . . isn't about war. It's about peace. It isn't about retaliation, it's about prevention. It isn't about fear, it's about hope, and in that struggle, if you will pardon my stealing a film line, the Force is with us.[7]

DEFENDING PEOPLE
OR MISSILE SILOS?

Star Wars I is still aloft. The American public is still encouraged to listen to its euphoric bleeps about a leakproof shield in the hereafter. But its functions are wholly ideological – to sell SDI and make it feel good. In the circle around the President the 'loyalty oath' still operates: it is obligatory to pretend that the government's aim is (in Weinberger's words) 'a thoroughly reliable and total' system of defence.

But as we have noted Star Wars I has run into atmospheric resistance. Even the government's own advisory panels, appointed in 1983 in the main from the weapons industries and laboratories, did not give to SDI unambiguous endorsement. James C. Fletcher, the chairman of one panel, dismissed the notion that SDI could defend the whole US population: 'Total is one thing, substantial is another . . . What you want is to minimize casualties. There is no such thing as a nuclear umbrella.' The other panel noted that even 'modest leaks' would be 'sufficient to destroy a very large part of our urban structure and population', and advised 'more modest' objectives – 'intermediate' systems designed to protect military targets.

The scepticism of the American scientific and technological community – or at least of those members of it who are independent of Pentagon-related retainers – was more profound. The radical Union of Concerned Scientists mounted an expert opposition, and the mainstream Federation of American Scientists attended, with equal expertise, to the consequences of SDI for arms control. Objections to Star Wars already noted in Chapter 2 were summarized in a letter to the *Wall Street Journal* (2 January 1985) from the Nobel laureate in physics, Hans A. Bethe, with five eminent fellow scientists (Richard L. Garwin, Kurt Gottfried, Henry W. Kendall, Carl Sagan and Victor Weisskopf). They set these down as *underflying* – getting under the shield with cruise missiles, low-altitude aircraft or SLBMs, or even 'suitcase bombs'; *overwhelming* – the saturation of defences by multiple attacks; *outfoxing* – decoys, penetration aids, the blinding of radar; *cost*; and *Soviet pre-emption* – the temptation of the Soviet military (or whoever may have been nominated as enemy in thirty years' time) to prevent a shield from being completed by 'retaliating first'.

While this debate was continuing, a great number of interests (military, aerospace industry, research, extremist Cold Warriors and uneasy diplomats trying to keep NATO allies in line) gathered around the project and tried to turn it to their own ends. *The New York Times*, early in 1985, identified four co-existing arguments for SDI, each of which contradicted the others:

The President and his aides have been selling Star Wars on four different, incompatible grounds: (1) It is the only moral defence in the nuclear age. (2) It is only research for our grandchildren. (3) It will soon be useful, indeed indispensable, even if imperfect. (4) It is a proven stimulus to arms control.

Argument (1) was for the American public, and sometimes for export to the rest of the world. Argument (2) was for objectors in Congress or in Europe, who feared that SDI would dismantle all treaties and end all arms control. Argument (4) – the 'bargaining chip' – was offered to Chancellor Kohl and Mrs Thatcher, to help them with their domestic critics. Argument (3) is the one which the military–industrial complex has bought, to lubricate any development whatsoever. All four arguments were supported by Argument (5): the Russians are doing it and at any time the bear may 'break out'.

By the end of 1984 it was clear to anyone who followed the United States press and congressional hearings – although not to the majority of

British and European commentators, who preferred to pass on US Information Service hand-outs – that Argument (3) was in the ascendant. Fred Iklé, US Under Secretary of Defense for Policy, told the Senate Armed Services Committee when in secret session in 1984:

It stands to reason that as you move toward deployment of the full system, there are some intermediate steps that have intermediate utility.

And 'components of a multi-tiered defence could become deployed earlier'. In April 1984 the Pentagon published a booklet which affirmed that 'between 1990 and 2000 the United States may decide to provide increasing protection for its allies and itself by deploying portions' of the SDI system.[8]

Such 'portions' relate to what is known in the jargon of the trade as 'point defence' or 'hard-site defence'. We are all in favour of defence. But what is the point of 'point defence'? And which points will be defended? Well . . . really *sensitive* targets, of course, like missile-silos, Strategic Air Command, NORAD's hollow mountain in Colorado, radar installations, and the arcana of state security and C^3I. Cities? People? Come on!

Such defences would cover small areas – perhaps thirty miles in radius. We are back with the old BMD systems, so long experimented with (and deployed around Moscow with the Galosh – p. 53) and lobbied for so eagerly by High Frontier. Such point defence makes better sense for missiles than for people, since even a leaky umbrella over a cluster of hardened missile silos might do all that was needed, in saving a percentage of them for a retaliatory second strike, whereas the defence of a city must be total or it is not defended at all. As Frank von Hippel of the Federation of American Scientists has argued:

Defence of . . . major cities against nuclear attack would be enormously more difficult than defending hard missile silos. Silo defence requires only having a moderate confidence of preventing up to a few nuclear warheads from coming very close to a silo for long enough to allow launch of its missiles. In contrast, city defence requires almost perfect success for the entire duration of the war in keeping thousands of hostile nuclear warheads miles away from targets which themselves cover tens of thousands of square miles.[9]

Or, in the more opaque language of one of the publications of the trade:

The system leakage, defined as the percent of targeted RVs [re-entry vehicles] that penetrate the defence, is classified as 'moderate'. Leakage is tolerable in any defence mission where a 100 per cent survival level is not required, such as the defence of hardened targets like missile silos.[10]

It follows that Mr Iklé's 'intermediate steps' fall a little short of the Star Wars I vision. For some years before the good folk of Middle America – or even of Washington DC – can sleep soundly in their beds in the knowledge that they are protected by an impermeable shield they will go through a period of 'intermediate utility' in which their missiles are protected but they are not. As Herbert Scoville, the president of the American Arms Control Association and a former deputy director of the CIA, has noted: 'What it [SDI] is doing is essentially defending missiles and command-and-control centres. It is not a protection of the people.'[11]

There need not be anything especially menacing in this. When Congress cut down on the number of MX missiles to be deployed, it was not surprising that a lobby should grow up for BMD defences around the remaining ones – presenting this as an instalment of SDI.[12] Missile silo defences don't appear at first sight to be more threatening than defences around airfields or submarine-bases, or than other stratagems to conceal or to harden what is always presented by the theorists as a second-strike or 'retaliatory' force.

But the matter was sensitive, and it was discussed at first in hushed tones. The sensitivity was, first of all, ideological. The President was still selling SDI as a defence of people: 'it's better to protect lives than to avenge them', as he told the American people in his weekly radio chat in July 1985, just before entering hospital for his cancer operation.[13] This did not look so good when it turned out that the first things to be defended were avenging nukes. Second, as we have seen, the elaboration of such missile defences would entail a break-out from the ABM Treaty. This takes us back once more into the looking-glass world of Mutual Assured Destruction or MAD.

FIRST-STRIKE FANTASIES

MAD and its various refinements, such as counterforce and NUTS (Nuclear Utilization Target Selection), have become a logic-spinning game in which armchair strategists tease out worst-case hypotheses in an endless series of abstract if-this-then-thats. The theorists probably have very little influence on actual military planning, and their theories nearly always arrive after the arrival of the weapons. Their language of 'credibility', 'posture' and 'perception', within the 'balance' of 'deterrence', supposes that great military powers are moved and checked within some rational chess game, in which the weapons are themselves players on the board, whereas the real and untidy threats to peace – Afghanistan, hostage crises, surges of nationalist hysteria – arise from areas for which their theory has no terms.

Yet deterrence theory is an ideological force in its own right, which influences politicians and publicists. In this world of mirrors, 'defence' and 'offence' are always changing places. Menacing ICBMs in their silos can suddenly be seen with pathos as pitifully exposed targets. It was out of this scholastic looking-glass world that the 'window of vulnerability' suddenly emerged: it seemed that the increasing accuracy of the new MIRVed (Multiple Independently Targeted Re-entry Vehicle) Soviet ICBMs (such as the SS-17, SS-18 and SS-19) might take out the American land-based missiles at any time. But this would 'destabilize' deterrence, by removing the threat of a second-strike or retaliatory force. This would therefore offer an incitement, in emergency, for a US first strike: the missiles must be out of their silos and away before the Soviet ICBMs homed in – the Americans must 'use them or lose them'. (According to this mirror-logic, Greenham Common is the most pitifully exposed sitting duck of them all, whose prototype was Pearl Harbor.)

MAD has now come to mean many things. It may refer to an outmoded strategic targeting policy, based on the mutual threat to cities and populations; or it may refer to a balance of terror and a state of approximate parity within which more refined targeting strategies may operate. But whether we call it MAD or not, the whole crazy superstructure of elaborating menace is justified in the name of 'deterrence'.

For years NATO warriors have been assuring us that deterrence theory has biblical authority. Mr Heseltine has told us that it is the only thing that, for thirty years, has held up the sky. But Star Wars I has called in question deterrence theory and, worse, described it as 'immoral'. And the more limited instalment of defending missile silos would introduce new tensions into 'deterrence'. For if American ICBMs are sheltering securely under shields there is no way in which Soviet ICBMs can target them and hence deter them. If the Soviet military perceive this as threatening, what are they likely to do? The first reflex might be to multiply their ICBMs in the hope of penetrating the shields. The second reflex might be to modify their targeting and return to the strategies of old-fashioned MAD: they would aim not at Grand Forks, Fort Warren and Greenham Common but at New York, Chicago and London instead. Hence, if we give any credence to deterrence theory, the 'intermediate' phase of Star Wars (which is all that we are ever likely to get) would make people, and not missiles, the target.

The Soviet military might, of course, as a third reflex, develop their own BMD shields. They already have the means to attempt this. But the 'intermediate utility' stations of point defence will disadvantage the USSR and advantage the USA. For Soviet land-based missiles have some thirty minutes to travel before they reach the United States. If we suppose the first BMD defences to be applied in the terminal phase (when the missiles are re-entering the atmosphere) then this will give time for satellite and radar identification and for accurate targeting. But US forward-based missiles in Europe, such as the Pershing IIs, must travel for only a few minutes. Hence this kind of ballistic missile defence might be more feasible for the USA than the USSR. For exactly the same reasons, it is also less feasible for Western Europe, against short or medium-range Soviet attack (e.g. SS-20s).

If we return to the President's unmodified vision of Star Wars I as a leakproof shield over the USA, then this shield would replace 'deterrence' with technology. But how would it get from A to B? In his launching speech of March 1983 Reagan himself sounded one note of caution:

> I clearly recognize that defensive systems have limitations and raise certain problems and ambiguities. If paired with offensive systems, they can be viewed as fostering an aggressive policy and no one wants that.

Yet this pairing of offensive and defensive planning has been exactly the posture of the United States in the past two years. In the first months of 1985 Reagan forced through Congress appropriations for a further instalment of MX missiles. According to one well-informed projection the current modernization of the US strategic arsenal will give –

- 1,500 air-launched cruise missiles, mainly on B-52 bombers (1,080 already deployed);

- uncertain numbers of sea-launched cruise missiles (a few already deployed);
- a further 1,500 advanced air-launched cruise missiles, to be deployed in late 1980s;
- a fleet of 100 B-1 bombers, to become operational by April 1988;
- a force of Stealth bombers, operational early 1990s;
- more than 25 Trident-class submarines (seven already operational), mainly armed with the accurate multi-warhead D-5 missile;
- an uncertain number of MX missiles (the first operational in late 1986);
- over 500 Midgetman missiles (partial deployment planned for 1992).

This inventory, which does not include forward-based missiles (such as ground-launched cruise and Pershing II) nor all the short-range ('tactical') stuff in the pipeline, looks somewhat offensive. And the Soviet military have modernized, or are modernizing, their own arsenal at a comparable pace. But, according to an American defence commentator:

> Pentagon officials avoid public discussion of the strategic balance between the United States and the Soviet Union that takes into account American modernization. Such officials much prefer an assessment that dwells exclusively on Soviet programmes in the hope of gaining congressional and public support . . .

But if these 'modernizations' are borne in mind, then in some seven years' time (i.e. when elements of SDI are projected to enter first deployments) the United States will probably have:

- a two-bomber strategic air arm designed to be able to penetrate the Soviet Union well into the twenty-first century;
- a supposedly invulnerable fleet of missile-launching submarines and a force of land-based intercontinental missiles with better, if imperfect, survivability;
- a substantially improved ability to destroy targets built to resist the effects of nuclear weapons, such as Soviet missile silos and command bunkers.[14]

This is, precisely, the offensive/defensive mix against which President Reagan warned. It is so provocative that, in this context, SDI can only be seen as the coping-stone set upon the carefully constructed edifice of outright American nuclear superiority.[15] With his right hand the President multiplies offensive weapons while with his left hand he proposes to eliminate the incoming Soviet ICBMs. SDI is simply a way of effecting unilateral measures of disarmament on the other side: Mr Reagan adds his own missiles up and crosses out a portion of the opponent's.

Inevitably this provokes a scary scenario of the United States getting ready to deliver a disarming first strike. Frank von Hippel has noted that 'such a system [SDI] makes much more sense as an adjunct to a first-strike capability than as a shield from a first strike'.[16] For if the United States were to meditate such a strike, in which its modernized and accurate armoury were to 'take out' the majority of Soviet ICBMs in their silos, *then* even a somewhat leaky Star Wars system might deal effectively with whatever second-strike capability was left in the shattered Soviet arsenal.

It is interesting to note that Edward Teller envisaged *precisely* this strategy as long ago as 1964, although of course it is a strategy which he imagines might be followed by the Russians:

... although I do not believe that a first strike would be likely to destroy all our Minutemen and submarines and Polarises, I think that it might be possible that a first strike would have greatly weakened our Minutemen and Polaris force – reduced this force to a fraction. If then the Russians had also introduced missile defence, it might turn out that this missile defence was sufficient to stop a retaliatory strike ... [17]

All this is worst-case hypothesis, the logic-spinning of deterrence theory. In any real world such a first-strike adventure would be crazily risky and, even if successful (which taxes all credibility), would expose aggressor and victim alike to the consequent nuclear winter.[18] Yet these ideological fictions are plausible enough to command huge resources and to set alarm-bells ringing in the heads of theorists and political leaders on the other side. For the name of the nuclear game – at least until the accident or political crisis which brings the Final Solution – is one of posture and prestige, 'face' and perceptions.[19]

The aim is to acquire such manifest evidences of 'superiority' that a first-strike would be *credible*. The strategists on the other side would then see a hole open in their heavens, a 'window of vulnerability'. The enemy would not know if the threat was bluff or not. At that point the United States could just 'take the Russians with a phone call'. As Reagan put it (but inverting, like Teller, the antagonists) if the Russians 'developed a defensive weapon before us, then they wouldn't have to worry about our deterrent . . . They could issue the ultimatum to the world.'[20] Tucked up in his chair at the Rancho del Cielo at Santa Barbara, the President has visions that the Force is with him, when he issues his own ultimatum:

Hi! Is that Gobashov? This is your President speaking, President of Planet Earth. Now pin your ears back, Gobchops! I want you Commies to come out with your hands up or I'll put the Force through your window. And don't think you can get in at *my* window 'cos I've got a good hickory board nailed across that. One . . . two . . . three . . .

FALL-OUT IN NATO

Star Wars did not really come to Europe until the President's re-election at the end of 1984, when it suddenly appeared that the man was in earnest. It seems that some of the Reaganauts supposed that the European NATO allies would fall about with gratitude at this new initiative, and would rush to Star Wars like pigs to slop. These governments, after all, had been through traumas during the Euro-missile crisis of 1981–3. The emergence of powerful peace movements – Edward Teller argued – signalled an end to popular consensus about 'deterrence' – a consensus (or torpor) upon which, in the end, all weapons (whether on sea, land or air) are based. If nothing were to be done to bring military strategy back into 'harmony' with public opinion, then Europe might default or even fall into the ultimate sin of unilateral disarmament.[21] Fred Iklé was goaded into uncustomary flights of eloquence by the same reflections. Revelations such as that of the 'nuclear winter' awaken 'deep anxieties', and the scheming Soviets 'could lay iron hands on the deepest emotions and fears of a great many people in the West'. By cunningly fanning this panic, Soviet manipulators might provoke demoralization and Western leaders could be forced by their own publics to make concessions.

Even the current deployment of intermediate-range missiles in Western Europe came close to being prevented by the combined pressures of Soviet manipulation and political opinion in the West. Had one of the West European elections turned out differently, the Soviet government would have succeeded in depriving the alliance of one of the supports it needed for deterrence.

Indeed Iklé feared, as did Teller, that MAD was rapidly losing the confidence of democratic opinion, and then the whole grandiloquent structure of weaponry and strategy would collapse amidst its own ruins:

Upon an alliance of democracies, such a policy [MAD] imposes a passive, almost cynical, resignation toward the possibility of an atrocity unsurpassed in human history. It offers a prospect of anxiety without relief, an intellectual legacy crippling the outlook of each new generation, a theme of desolate sadness . . . To insist that only a rigorously preserved vulnerability will preserve us from annihilation is a credo that must corrode the confidence upon which civilizations are built.[22]

– thus the melancholy anti-nuclear philosopher who, in his working hours, is condemned to slave at a desk in the Pentagon, as Under Secretary of Defense for Policy, justifying the greatest nuclear preparations known to the world.

It followed from these arguments that America's allies in Europe would be the first to see the need for an 'alternative to deterrence' which would reverse the rising tide of anti-nuclear feeling. But the reaction of the satellite NATO governments fell short of gratitude. They do not have two oceans between them and the Other. They shared the theory of deterrence, but gave it a regional accent. West Europe is supposed to be, already, under an umbrella of US (and some British and French) ICBMs. This umbrella – NATO's strategists have always argued – keeps out not only Soviet nukes but also Soviet conventional forces, since NATO has persistently warned that it reserves the option of a first nuclear strike against attack by conventional forces. Furthermore, NATO's European allies had only just survived the traumas of forcing down their public's throats unwanted cruise and Pershing II missiles, by touting them from the media's rooftops for their restorative properties in giving back to Europe, once more, an umbrella.

Star Wars made monkeys of the loyal NATO governments and their attendant defence experts. As Colonel Alford, of the International Institute for Strategic Studies, told *The New York Times*: 'Europeans actually tend to like nuclear weapons.'[23] By this we must suppose that the good colonel did not refer to those Europeans who demonstrate against missiles or who answer opinion polls, but to another species of loyal Europeans – *Homo europæus philatlanticus* – who staff the military services, defence ministries and the institutes for strategic research. This species really does 'like' the Bomb. They have persuaded themselves that 'the deterrent' truly is the only thing that prevents a major European war.

The belief in 'deterrence' is not dishonourable: and if accompanied (as it rarely is) by genuine attempts to secure disarmament to minimal levels and to encourage international reconciliation, it is compatible with the pursuit of peace. But the True Believers, who were the chorus who welcomed in cruise, were utterly confounded by Star Wars. They suspected that SDI signalled a strategic retreat which would de-couple Europe from Fortress America. If America alone had an SDI shield, and could launch its missiles with impunity, they feared this might encourage American adventurism or could lead to a 'limited' nuclear war being fought in Europe. Or if the Soviet Union built a shield also, then Europe would be left as a no-man's-land between the superpowers, with the laser-zapped nukes of both sides falling on its head.

Moreover, as the *Guardian* asked in a leader (5 February 1985), if both superpowers were protected by 'domes', 'What thereafter becomes of the British and French nuclear deterrents?' The answer (which the *Guardian* unaccountably overlooked) is that we could point them across the Channel and use them to deter each other. But NATO's first-use nuclear guarantee would expire, and this would make 'the world safe for conventional war'. This was noted by Professor Michael Howard, and his words were echoed by a wizard in the French Foreign Ministry: 'Making the world safe for conventional war is not at all appealing for Europeans.'[24] And if the Russians had a shield, then all those lovely nukes, including the French Hades and our own putative Trident, would cease overnight to be 'deterrents' to the USSR and would become only irritants. This irritated Mrs Thatcher so much that, with uncustomary temerity, she allowed herself (when Mr Gorbachov visited London early in December 1984) to come forward with him at a joint press conference at which they both expressed their opposition to an arms race in space.

The effect upon the White House was sensational. For Mrs Thatcher to appear together with a leading Commie and to criticize (by implication) the President's pet project was regarded as petty treason. But when the President rang London to sound off, the line had gone dead. Mrs Thatcher was at that moment following in the wake of Sir Francis Drake and circumnavigating the globe. She was like a satellite in orbit, travelling widdershins around Planet Earth, on her way to Peking, Hong Kong, and thence to Washington and to a lunch date with

President Reagan at Camp David. The President's cables caught up with her at length in Honolulu. She was told that she must either eat her words or she must get her lunch in a MacDonalds. Mrs Thatcher ate her words, first in public in an interview with BBC Radio Four on board her RAF VC-10, and then in private with the President, who had them served up to her like sausages on a waffle.[25]

In return for her renewed fealty, President Reagan issued to all his European allies a very large public waffle to the effect that the impermeable shield (which had now become both a dome and an umbrella) was going to be extended to them also. This nonsensical promise was not worth the spit that issued with it, but the loyal NATO governments and their servile media, for a week or two, swam happily around in the spittoon.

Mrs Thatcher's capitulation was dressed up by the PR people with the grand name of the Camp David Accords. The President and the Prime Minister were supposed to have reached complete agreement on Star Wars, provided that four 'principles' were observed: (1) the aim is not to achieve superiority but to maintain balance; (2) research could go ahead, but any deployment must await consultation and superpower negotiation (i.e. revision or abrogation of the ABM Treaty); (3) the overall aim is to enhance, not to undercut, deterrence; (4) SDI research must go along with negotiations to reduce offensive systems on both sides. It is not clear whether Mr Reagan was listening to Maggie's Accords, since he was humming to himself and looking out of the window. The Accords were gift-wrapped and brought back on the VC-10 to Downing Street (where European visitors were invited to admire them) but nothing more was heard about them from the White House.

So far as the Reaganauts were concerned, all that the Camp David Accords meant was that Maggie had been whipped back in line. Their interpretation was that the British government would give public support to SDI, provided that the US did not move to the stage of deployment, in contravention of the ABM Treaty, without prior negotiation. When Mrs Thatcher revisited Washington and addressed Congress (20 February) she was dripping with unction. 'Mr President, we in Britain think you're wonderful!' she assured Reagan (and the cameras) at a banquet, to the nausea of the British viewing public. Her speech 'was widely interpreted in the United States as offering almost unqualified backing' to Star Wars.[26]

But what about the waffle? In the launch speech of March 1983, President Reagan had added on to his original draft the aim of protecting the United States 'or her allies'. It seems that when the Force is with him, Reagan is able to extend his shield at will: to Europe, to Israel, to Japan (although never to the Third World). If the cost of raising a leaky umbrella over the American nation would be out of this world, the cost of extending it from Iceland and Norway to Turkey would be out of this galaxy. But the offer proved the goodness of Ronald Reagan's heart. So far as we can establish, the offer has not been supported by a single feasibility study.

There are only two ways in which the offer could make even hypothetical half-sense. The first could be proposals (perhaps made to Mrs Thatcher in private) that the United States could extend ABM point defences to strategic bases in Europe – especially US missile bases such as Greenham Common and Molesworth. Mr Heseltine could then run happily up and down in his flak jacket at the head of thousands of troops, chasing the last Quaker, in the secure knowledge that he was under an American shield.

Even so, there would be a small political cost for this shield. Two authors have pointed out that while interceptor systems against intermediate-range missiles (such as SS-20s) might just be feasible in Europe, the interceptors 'would have as little as three to ten minutes to detect, identify, track, target and attack incoming warheads'. This would require 'an automated and automatic US ABM response', such as LOW (launch-on-warning). 'There will be no time to work through NATO's established consultative channels. European political authorities thus will be effectively removed from any active role in decisions concerning nuclear war on their own soil.' [27] One had supposed that this was the case already, but there is a finality about automating the process. The 'dome' turns out to be an automated system for the extinction of European autonomy.

The other hypothetical means of extending the dome to cover Europe lies in the exotic technology proposed to intercept Soviet ICBMs in their boost phase (pp. 31–2). If this – the most far-fetched and controversial element of the system – were to come off, then the ICBMs would be zapped before their targeting could be known, and hence, willy-nilly, the dome would be extended, not only to Europe, but also to Kampuchea, Iraq and Morocco: in fact, to any territory within range. So taken were White House advisers with this notion that they began to tout it to Europe as new evidence of US altruism. Dr Keyworth invited Europeans to think of SDI, not as a protective dome over themselves, but as a dome (or lid) placed over the Soviet Union, to prevent their missiles from getting out.[28]

Even the True Believers in Europe have been sceptical of this notion, although they have been careful to speak in hushed voices lest their own publics should overhear. The unmannerly French have even been sardonic. This is not only because they are sceptical of the technology and alert to the likely leakage if it were ever put in place. It is also because the most evident threat to Europe comes not from ICBMs but from aircraft, cruise missiles, artillery, medium-range missiles (SS-20s), and low-trajectory short-range missiles such as the SS-21s, SS-22s and SS-23s. While some of these might be brought down by surface-to-air interceptors, no competent military adviser would entrust the future of his country to such problematic methods. MAD still seemed to be the only viable defence. By the first months of 1985 an extraordinary and unwished-for railway accident seemed to be about to take place in the marshalling yards of the NATO alliance. A venture which had been set in motion to checkmate the Soviets and turn the tables on the peace movement was turning out to be a nasty diplomatic encounter between America and her loyal NATO allies.

EUROPE: THE PORK-BARREL OR SALT?

At the time of writing, United States administration response to the truculence of Europeans has gone through two phases. In the first phase, from January to May 1985, there has been an extraordinary PR operation to sell them Star Wars I. The means have varied from smooth sales-talk to material enticements (suggestions of lucrative research contracts) to plain ultimatums. In the second phase (from May until ?) the Europeans have been offered a modified SDI: Star Wars II. God knows what the next stage will be.

In the first stage, couriers shuttled across the Atlantic – Caspar Weinberger (several times), Mr Reagan himself, General Abrahamson, Edward Teller, and a score of underlings – and several attempts were made to get meetings of NATO Foreign or Defence Ministers to pronounce their loyalty to SDI. All were unsuccessful. The French were haughtily independent. President Mitterrand did not mince his words: SDI was speculative, its consequences would be destabilizing, it would provoke an arms race in space and damage the prospects for disarmament. 'NATO's main interest must be to remain true to nuclear deterrence,' declaimed Charles Hernu, the Defence Minister, maintaining the long-established French tradition of prompting NATO on its duties from outside.[29] The Danes and, subsequently, the Norwegians refused participation, as did Australia.[30] The West Germans vacillated, as did the Dutch, as splits began to open up within the governing coalitions: Chancellor Kohl liked SDI, but his coalition partner, the Foreign Minister Herr Genscher, liked it less.[31] 'One of the worst problems we're having . . . is with the allies,' a 'high State Department official' told *The New York Times* in March: 'And it only looks as if we have it under control for the moment.'[32]

A major response to this truculence was for the White House to play the 'SS-20 card': that is, to demand the allegiance of allies because the Soviet Union was already streaking ahead in ABM and space-based researches, not to mention death rays of all kinds. Measures touted as innocent and peaceful, if taken by the USA, became terrible threats if taken by the Soviets. European governments were inundated with briefings about Soviet developments in space. The supposed 'ABM gap' (Chapter 3) was discovered, and whenever European defence correspondents lifted the telephone they heard heavy breathings of Soviet threat, relayed by courtesy of US information services. They were told that the Soviets were just about to break out of the ABM Treaty. They were just about to deploy their own SDI. The sinister phased-array radar near Krasnoyarsk (pp. 55, 87) did duty for the SS-20s. Finally, early in March, President Reagan turned up the volume control. Taking the gospel (and the shield) to Canada he announced that the Soviet Union was now violating the ABM Treaty, and (for good measure) the SALT II agreements, the Geneva Convention on chemical warfare, and the Yalta and Helsinki agreements.

Even Whitehall could now see what was coming. The way in which a treaty is abrogated, or a new weapons system is commissioned, is always to set up a cry that the other side is doing it or that, if we don't, then they will. This has been done by both sides, and there usually is something to point to in the Other. In this case, the USSR, just like the USA, had been pressing forward in the 'grey areas' of the ABM Treaty. But the orchestration of official US indignation was a clear indication that the President was making the case for an early US break-out or abrogation of the 1972 treaty. Worse than that, he was on the verge of breaking out of those nicely packaged Camp David Accords.

It was in these circumstances that the British blew a fuse, and the name of the fuse was the Foreign Minister, Sir Geoffrey Howe. On 15 March 1985 he delivered at the Royal United Services Institute a temperate and reasoned speech whose essence was a defence of the classic tenets of 'deterrence'. In their name he defended the ABM Treaty and recalled the British interpretation of the Camp David Accords. He reaffirmed British support for 'research' into SDI technologies, but warned that 'research may acquire an unstoppable momentum of its own':

We must take care that political decisions are not pre-empted by the march of technology, still less by premature attempts to predict the route of the march.

He noted that SDI might be matched by counter-measures, and warned against 'creating a new Maginot Line . . . liable to be outflanked by relatively simpler and demonstrably cheaper counter-measures'. Would the defences not 'inexorably crank up the levels of offensive nuclear systems designed to overwhelm them'? And he lightly hinted at the strains which SDI imposed upon the NATO alliance.

Sir Geoffrey's speech scarcely moved beyond the elaboration of the Accords which Mrs Thatcher supposed that she had agreed with President Reagan at Camp David ten weeks before. But the response to the speech was sensational. For some reason *The Times* of London had become the leading organ in Europe for Star Wars I advocacy, and one which revealed extraordinarily close – even intimate – briefings which appeared to come directly from the White House. On 18 March Sir Geoffrey was subjected to an attack, in a very long leader ('Howe's UDI from SDI') of extraordinary vehemence. Habit-formed *Times* readers no doubt nodded through it with satisfaction, under the impression that it was directed, not at Sir Geoffrey Howe, but at Mr Arthur Scargill. The mild-mannered Sir Geoffrey was accused of using 'Luddite language'. The speech was 'mealy-mouthed, muddled in conception, negative, Luddite, ill-informed and, in effect if not intention, a "wrecking amendment" to the whole plan' of SDI. The speech had done 'untold damage to the cohesion of the Atlantic Alliance', and (for the Editor had already heard from the White House) had 'caused astonishment and pained reaction in the inner circle of the American administration'. It would help Mr Gorbachov to 'drive a wedge' between Europe and America. 'Whatever they may say in public, the Americans in private are not amused.'

In the next few days the air was full of official denials that anyone was upset and of telltale signals that they were.[33] The US Ambassador made a formal call on the Foreign Secretary and demanded back the gift-wrappings on the Camp David Accords. A more astonishing episode unrolled in the Royal Garden Hotel in London, where a 'Committee for the Free World' brought together into one assembly all the hawks of Europe and America to discuss 'Beyond 1984'. Lord Chalfont launched the proceedings by describing Sir Geoffrey's speech as a 'sad concoction of out-of-date slogans'. The assembly received messages of support from Mrs Thatcher and President Reagan, and was addressed by Ms Jeanne Kirkpatrick, America's outgoing Ambassador to the United Nations, who 'hoped and prayed' that the Geneva arms talks would fail. Dr Roger Scruton singled out the Foreign Office and Balliol College as sources of 'treachery'. All this was predictable.

But then Richard Perle, Reagan's serving Assistant Secretary of Defense, arose and roasted the British Foreign Secretary in his turn. Perle, who has earned the title of the 'Prince of Darkness' from his fierce opposition to arms-control agreements, and who played a notable part in wrecking the first Geneva talks on Euromissiles, had been leading the campaign for a unilateral US abrogation of the ABM Treaty.[34] Now he accused the Soviet Union of 'hippocrasy (*sic*) of Orwellian dimensions' and of 'out-and-out' and 'blatant' violation of arms treaties. He said that Sir Geoffrey's speech proved that 'length is no substitute for depth', and questioned 'in a manner that is both tendentious and obliquely declaratory, the strategic-defence programme of the United States'.[35] Whatever protocols the Soviet Union may have breached, for a serving minister in the American administration to attack the Foreign Secretary of a major ally in his own capital city broke all normal diplomatic proprieties.[36]

By now it was clear that something strange was going on. In the Euromissile crisis, the United States government (and their publicists) had secured the loyal commitment of most West European establishments and had carried the political centre (in politics and the media) as well as the Right. This time the hawks in the US administration were attempting to impose the same Atlanticist allegiance upon Europe by enlisting the support of ardent Cold Warriors and the 'loony Right'.

Both the Heritage Foundation and High Frontier entered the export business. An office in London with the pretentious name of the Institute for European Defence and Strategic Studies (director, Mr Gerald Frost) turns out – surprise! – to be 'associated with the Heritage Foundation'. (Mr Frost has been a zealous advocate of SDI.)[37] And a European High Frontier Advisory Council has been formed, with the support of the 'father' of the French H-Bomb, General Pierre Gallois; the Council's British representative is Air Vice-Marshal Stewart Menaul.[38]

Yet the work of this well-funded lobby did not prosper. The Star Warriors hoped to re-enact the dramas of 1980 to 1983, with governments and media clobbering the peace movements and the soft-on-the-Soviets Left – but now in the name of anti-nuclear morality. But sweat broke out on the brow of the European establishment when it contemplated going through all that again. Moreover, to do them justice, in addition to their firm belief in 'deterrence', many in the centre had hoped that the Geneva talks might succeed in lowering tensions and in reducing (or at least controlling) arms. The Atlantic became wider, and contradictions between the strategic and economic interests of both shores became more evident. What had been in Europe a pro-Atlanticist centre began to be replaced by a fringe lobby of space-fic millenarians, orchestrated by Reagan's groupies.

The climax and collapse of Star Wars promotion (phase one) came with a blunder by Caspar Weinberger. It had been noted in Washington that the soft spot in Europe's defences against Star Wars might be greed: the desire to get a cut of the $26 billions projected for research in the next five years. The West Germans seemed willing to be seduced; Mrs Thatcher made a shameless bid for pickings from the pork barrel when she addressed Congress in February 1985; and the Japanese (to whom President Reagan generously extended a shield) also showed an initial interest. The US administration has long been used to lobbying for its arms procurements on 'the Hill' by offering juicy contracts to the states of compliant Senators, and it saw an opportunity of extending the same technique from Arizona or Colorado to the petty (and unrepresented) states of Europe. As one shrewd American bureaucrat remarked, if European government support could not be bought, it still might be 'rented'.[39]

Mr Weinberger therefore thought that it would concentrate NATO's mind – and also the minds of Japan, Australia, South Korea and Israel – if he sent to the Defence Ministers of these states a letter inviting them to submit their applications to come in on the project:

I would ask, as a first step, that you send me, within sixty days, an indication of your interest in participating in the SDI research programme and the areas of your country's research excellence that you deem most promising . . .

This did indeed concentrate NATO's mind. It infuriated slow-moving government bureaucracies, and was taken as an 'ultimatum', an 'unsatisfactory way to deal with allies'. Within three weeks Caspar Weinberger was forced to withdraw his deadline. But scarcely had the allies settled their ruffled feathers before a new blast disordered them again. The Reaganauts were gathering their forces to break out of the surviving arms-control treaties once more. There was much scurrying across the Atlantic again, Mr Kissinger joining the Star Wars couriers. It suddenly became evident that Reagan was on the edge of renouncing the limits upon weaponry imposed by the (unratified but informally observed) SALT II agreement. And also that sharp in-fighting had developed within the US administration.

Since we have no access to White House keyholes we cannot identify the factions. Clearly Weinberger, Perle, and Iklé, with General Abrahamson and William Casey of the CIA belonged to the arms-control breakout faction, and hoped to carry Reagan with them. Someone in Washington later told *The Times* that this faction –

believe that strategic defence research is a matter of principle, almost a moral imperative, that should be pitched towards its highest potential, rather than be regarded mainly in a secondary context as an additional means of protecting retaliatory forces.[40]

The other faction was led by Mr George Shultz, the Secretary of State. No doubt the State Department had belatedly recognized that NATO was being placed under extreme tensions, and argued that the political cost of this was higher than SDI merited.

Mr Shultz, in his unassertive way, organized a resistance to the Star Warriors, and enlisted the NATO allies to bring him reinforcements to Washington. In the last week of May 1985 the President was expected to announce the abrogation of SALT II in view of Soviet 'violations'. He was persuaded to delay his decision for one week. In the interval the Senate voted by ninety to five to call on the President not to abandon the SALT limits. On 6 June the NATO Foreign Ministers gathered at Estoril in Portugal. Mr Shultz was able to take back to Washington a unanimous recommendation from the other NATO ministers that the United States continue to abide by both SALT II and the ABM Treaty. But he failed in his attempt to take with him also, as a sweetener, some general communiqué of approval for SDI. Reagan submitted to these overwhelming pressures and postponed his final decision on the treaties until November 1985. And that was the end of Star Wars I.[41]

STAR WARS MARK II OR EUREKA?

But by this time Star Wars II had long been sent aloft. This was a less moral but more practical model, modified for European conditions. Star Wars II does not offer to abolish nuclear weapons, it offers to 'enhance deterrence'. It no longer pretends to be leakproof. It will stop enough Russian ICBMs from getting out to confuse and 'frustrate' the Russians. It will make them 'uncertain' as to the likely success of a disarming first strike. Point defences at silo sites will further defend the NATO 'retaliatory' forces. Even if it is true that West Europe could not be defended as well as the United States, the 'enhancement' of US deterrence would frustrate Soviet aggressive designs and this would improve European security. And Star Wars II is marketed as a 'response' to Soviet ABM developments. It is only about 'research', and about the big money that goes with it.

Mark II was sent aloft with headlines such as 'Reagan Reshapes Star War Proposal'.[42] In fact Mark II is a sales brief drawn up by US military, diplomatic and national-security officials, and the credit for the blueprint might be given more to Mrs Thatcher, for it follows closely the principles of the Camp David Accords (p. 108).

The revamping of SDI in this form was a profound disappointment to the editor of *The Times*. It would relegate its 'radical potential to the dustbin':

If strategic defence is reduced to a mechanism which simply contributes to a defence of missile sites ... it would serve no greater purpose than any new weapons system. It would preserve the uncomfortable – indeed untenable – instability of today's nuclear doctrine, called Mutual Assured Destruction (MAD).[43]

For once we agree with *The Times*. Star Wars II is simply a new dimension to the nuclear arms race – on land, sea and air, and now in space.

At the end of June 1985 salesman-in-chief Vice-President Bush was sent off on an eleven-day, seven-nation tour of West Europe to get assent to Star Wars II. He anticipated no problems, since the European NATO establishment had long been MAD. Gone now were the millenarial promises of Star Wars I, unless as peroration and utopia. Mr Bush reassured his audiences that SDI was 'purely and simply a research programme', with possible deployments 'years off'. It was 'farthest' from American thinking to interfere with deterrence.[44] But, once again, the Vice-President went back to America empty-handed. This was partly because the luckless Mr Bush was, as always, upstaged by events. His show was stolen by the grand spectacular of the hostages crisis in the Lebanon. But it was also because the West Europeans were now preoccupied with the launch of a little space satellite of their own: Eureka.

Eureka was designed and patented by the French. As early as February 1984, President Mitterrand had made a speech at The Hague calling for a Western European response to the space challenge, the pooling of European knowhow in space researches, and the construction of a European orbiting space station. These proposals were reactivated by the French representative at a conference in Rome (30–31 January 1985), with increasing emphasis on the need to secure the competitiveness of European high-tech industries. The Germans and the British backed away, fearing to offend their American guardians, and wary of Gaullist ambitions to assume a French hegemony in Europe.

But then (15 March) Sir Geoffrey Howe made his own (almost-Gaullist) speech. On 18 April President Mitterrand was reading it in his bath (for the mail between London and Paris is slow), when he leapt out with the cry, *Eureka*! But to explain what Mitterrand thought he had found must take us into different (if equally murky) regions. Weinberger's memorandum to his NATO underlings had emphasized that the US Defense Department was already searching for European participation in the project. At first sight this 'rent' or bribe looked attractive, although generous estimates suggested that at the most $1 billion might pass across the Atlantic to European firms of the $26 billions projected for research in the next five years.[45] But at second sight it did not look as good. The NATO European military and arms contractors recalled the long record of US refusal of European wares and preference for their own.[46] The West Germans, in particular, recalled the row about the gas pipeline from the Soviet Union. Since the invasion of Afghanistan the United States had been trying to embargo the export of advanced technology to the Soviet Union, and had used a discipline of licences and punitive trading methods which often favoured the competition of American firms. Indeed, the embargo had extended to the whole Communist world. In 1984 MBB (Messerschmitt-Bölkow-Blohm) had arranged to sell a radio-TV satellite to China, but the United States refused a licence because this contained American parts. Subsequently an American firm moved in on the contract.[47] Other European firms, including British, had experienced the same restrictions.

The Germans had experienced an even more ominous example of the American determination to control high technology. *Der Spiegel* reported at the end of 1984 that the Americans had refused a licence to export from the United States an advanced computer made by Control Data to the prestigious Max Planck Institute in Hamburg (to be used in climatological research). In this case there was no question of the computer's export to the Communist world. But the United States demanded, as a condition of export, that every scientist in the Institute with access to the computer must go through the highest security vetting procedures – and should be banned from travelling to the Communist countries. Since it is normal, in a scientific research institute, for scientists at other universities to have access to major facilities, this American security screening could have reached far into the scientific community. Each time the computer was used a detailed document as to the user and purposes was to be completed and returned to American security. These conditions were rejected, as an infringement of the West German constitution.[48]

With such examples in mind, the Germans and the French began to look more closely into what part Europeans were being offered in SDI researches. Would it be as partners or as subcontractors, would there be a two-way exchange of technology or a security cage around even their own work? In March 1985, someone told *The Times*, the West German government informed the United States that they would cooperate in SDI if they had 'full access to all existing and future American technology, joint control of the programme of research and development, and joint operational controls of any system'.[49] No doubt the report is exaggerated. No one in Bonn can have been as innocent as *that*! But whatever terms were asked they proved to be too high.

The French were meditating on the same problem, of which they also had experience. And some of Mitterrand's ministers (who still remembered their socialist origins) came up with a remarkable, and by no means silly, hypothesis. Perhaps Star Wars is not, except in marginal ways, about military questions at all? And perhaps it is aimed less at the Soviet Union than at America's competitors in Europe and Japan?

The hypothesis has been argued lucidly by M. Claude Cheysson, former Foreign Minister and now a European Commissioner. He identified three objectives of United States policy: (1) to make American ICBM sites invulnerable; (2) to promote (in the President's eyes) a good moral image of the USA; (3) – and the most important –

In the name of the threat which they pretend hangs over the United States and Europe, it will be possible to inject considerable sums into scientific and technological research. The Americans wish in this way to recover their leadership in certain areas of the high technology of tomorrow.

But such measures of state investment are politically impossible in America owing 'to the sacred rules of the market economy'. Hence this investment requires a justification which overrides those rules, in the name of 'safeguarding the Free World'. The American taxpayer is to be stampeded into subsidizing private capitalist ends through the 'hysteria' of the Cold War.[50]

Seen in this light, the aim of SDI is not to 'enhance deterrence' but to enhance the competitiveness and technological supremacy of United States industry. It is a means of organizing research and development to the decisive advantage of the USA into the twenty-first century, so that both economic and security controls would ensure a one-way traffic. This was what President Mitterrand thought he had found when he read Howe's speech in his bath. The British might be brought round; West Europe needed its own SDI; but, instead of dressing it up as a military space programme, why not cut the cackle and go directly for the objective – the stimulation of technological research in its own right?

Eureka was thus sent aloft, as an answer to SDI, but not as an alternative defence system. At first it seemed that it would not lift off its pad. The British turned their back on it; there was a frosty exchange between Mitterrand and Chancellor Kohl, and the Paris–Bonn axis seemed to be endangered.[51] Then Caspar Weinberger's ultimatum began to turn European feeling. And both governments and leading industrialists began to feel alarm as General Abrahamson's SDI Organization sent scores of experts and advisers through European universities, laboratories and industrial plants.[52] The governments felt themselves being bypassed. It was feared that there would be a 'brain drain' of European professorial mercenaries to Livermore and Los Alamos.[53] It was feared that US merchants would simply hire whatever they could not get at home and put nothing back. When the Heriot-Watt University in Edinburgh received one of the first publicly announced contracts for Star Wars research in Europe ($150,000 for optical computers, with more perhaps to follow), there was an audible sniff from the Dutch giant, Philips: 'We would never accept such an order.' The British would get 150,000 dollars for their invention, while giving millions of dollars' worth of knowledge to the Americans. It might be all right for academics to give away research like that, but industry researched in order to *produce*.[54] The SDIO operators began to look more and more like asset-strippers; as one German scientist said, they were trying to 'pick out the raisins'.[55] With increasing resentment, other nations took up the French cry – they were being offered the role of 'subcontractors'. West Europe began to know what it is like to be in the Third World.

That is why, in the summer of 1985, substantial opinion rallied to Eureka, and at length West Germany and even Britain agreed to come in. We do not intend to extend this essay by speculating upon the future of Eureka, for the simple reason that by the time this book is published the readers will know more about that future than we do now. At the time of writing, Eureka is still an expression of intentions and a jostle of competing interests. We will content ourselves with certain caveats as to its peaceful configurations.

Eureka was launched as a programme of civil research, and its non-military intent was signalled by the participation of four neutral nations (Sweden, Finland, Switzerland and Austria). (It was unfortunate that Bulgaria should have also expressed an interest, and suggested that Eureka be extended 'from the Atlantic to the Urals' – it had never been intended that the research should be as civil as that.)[56] The project may even succeed in being civil in orientation, and in getting to its objectives more quickly than if it was waiting, as with SDI, for civil spin-offs from esoteric military research. But it should be noted that the research priorities of both Eureka and SDI run closely parallel to each other. The French proposals for Eureka were at first 'a faithful copy' of the research priorities of SDI: micro-electronics, advanced computers, artificial intelligence, optical electronics, lasers and particle-energy beams, and new materials.[57] These were later modified, with the addition of robotics (and 'automated factories') and bio-technologies.[58] The civil emphasis has thereby been strengthened.

Yet if there is spin-off in one way there will be spin-off in the other. A Dutch correspondent noted that 'for purely political–psychological reasons the French fall silent when they are asked about the military spin-off' from Eureka. But it is clear that this will be generated.[59] Anthony Tucker, the *Guardian*'s science editor, has pointed out that Eureka's drive for fifth- or sixth-generation computers, capable of thirty Gigaflops a second, is unlikely to 'widen Europe's grip on world markets', since the market for such machines 'will scarcely run into double figures'. The main users of such machines will be the military, and Tucker asks if Eureka is 'a cover for military developments whose cost would otherwise be wholly unacceptable'.[60]

The attempt to make a strict distinction between European and American arms contractors can be strained too far. There is too much integration between multinationals for this to be made. Philips (which backs Eureka) has American subsidiaries, like Magnavox, which are in touch with the SDIO.[61] According to General Abrahamson, the French Thomson-Csf (a partner of CGE) supplies the klystron tubes used in most American lasers.[62] The French giant, MATRA, has collaborated with Rockwell, United Technologies and TRW in America for twenty years. Although it is 51 per cent owned by the French state, it will contract for both SDI and Eureka if the terms are good.[63] So also, it is probable, will British Aerospace, Italian Selenia and the Bavarian MBB. Indeed, MBB (Messerschmitt-Bölkow-Blohm) has shown a sense of duty to its shareholders: 'We deliver political services. If we get an order for SDI we shall carry it out.'[64] The 'political services' of Messerschmitt in two world wars are still remembered.

There is a 'footbridge' between SDI and Eureka, across which the military contractors can pass.[65] Moreover the traffic passes more easily because adherents of a free market economy – notably Chancellor Kohl and Mrs Thatcher – can pretend that arms contracting, like any business, is strictly a private affair. Great Britain, also known as *perfide*

Albion, is playing both ends against the middle: coming in on Eureka (in case there are any pickings there) while sending Mr Heseltine to Washington (in the name of the 'special relationship') in the hope of favours from SDI.[66]

What forms, apart from contracts, might the military spin-off from Eureka take? One obvious form is the development of more lethal high-tech conventional arms.[67] Another (noted especially by the French) would be point defences of their own aerodromes, bases and 'deterrents'. General Gallois has even suggested that 'certain' industrially advanced countries 'which have renounced nuclear arms' (or are barred by their constitutions from possessing them) 'such as Japan and Germany' could 'recover their military power' by jumping the nuclear stage and going directly to lasers and other forms of death ray.[68] It is a happy thought.

We cannot peer into that murky future. Eureka does indicate a gesture of independence from Washington, a refusal to be a mere subcontractor to SDI. But it could also be a political subterfuge. As 'some French officials' told *The New York Times*, it is 'a way to better negotiate "Star Wars" contracts while avoiding a direct political endorsement' of SDI.[69] The American salesmen, after their initial anger, have adjusted their tactics to this subterfuge. They continue to pick out the 'raisins' from the European cake. They continue to have powerful friends (like Lord Chalfont and Franz Josef Strauss), who advocate full European commitment to SDI. And there is some talk now of trying to divert Eureka into a kind of regional SDI. In this division of labour (and of costs), Europe would have its special responsibilities and some control over its own technologies, in a Tactical Defence Initiative, or TDI.[70] Eureka cannot be trusted as a 'civil' research programme unless it is given a quite new political content and direction. Otherwise even its civil spin-offs may be desolate. As the Dutch Labour Party has noted, the prospectus for Eureka offers no social objectives and is innocent of even one 'social paragraph'. High technology and competitiveness are assumed as unexamined goals. But do we really wish our enterprises (and even our intelligence) to be 'robotized' and the human species to be made redundant by software?[71]

Why, in view of the opposition of their closest friends of yesterday, has Washington gone on and on thrusting Star Wars down Europe's throat until it sicked up Eureka as a protest? Is it just plain superpower ego-tripping? Ideological macho? The need to impose allegiance (in the name of NATO 'unity') upon their client states once more? If we leave 'research' aside, it has been suggested that an explanation might be found in military logistics.[72] If ABM defences are to be developed for the United States, the further forward these are based the better. George Keyworth, the President's science adviser, has said: 'The technology is likely to require some bases in Europe . . . Some systems will have to be in Europe.'[73] What systems will these be?

Very clearly, the existing advanced sensing, tracking and targeting installations, as well as communications control generally, will have to be very much developed. This will involve ABM radar in Europe of the kind currently prohibited in the ABM Treaty (p. 88). New radar installations are now being built by the United States in Canada, Greenland and Iceland, and Mr Weinberger reported to the US Congress (without consulting the British government) that work would commence on a phased-array radar at Fylingdales in Yorkshire in 1986 (p. 88).[74] No one has yet informed Congress that ICBM interceptor missiles or other SDI hardware will be based on the territory of NATO allies, although Mr Weinberger told a Canadian TV interviewer: 'I don't have any idea as to where the defences might be placed . . . We would try to . . . locate the best places for defences. Some might be here [in Canada], some might be in the United States, some might be at sea. It just depends on where the most effective technical place for them to be put is.'[75]

A very 'effective technical place' will be Canada and Europe: on the northern rim (Iceland, Norway) across the North Pole, just possibly in Israel or Sicily, and very probably in special-relationship Britain. As we have seen (p. 32) the Star Warriors are now keen on 'pop-up' laser systems, instead of keeping vulnerable space platforms in permanent orbit. In an alert these would pop up (from land or submarines) to identify, target or attack Soviet ICBMs climbing in their boost phase. But to do this they must be able to 'see' over the curvature of the planet's rim. In the space-fic scenarios of Star Wars the advantages of forward-basing are very significant. According to General Gallois, to fire a laser from US territory would require popping up mirrors, with extreme speed, to an altitude of about 2,000 kilometres, whereas to intercept short or medium-ranged missiles, 'pop-ups' could be lofted from West Europe to a height of only 20–80 km.[76]

From forward-basing, further consequences would follow. The decisive element of SDI will be C^3I: the instant processing of incoming signals and the almost-simultaneous emission of multitudes of targeting instructions. To the embarrassment of PR at the White House, Mr Fred Iklé, when in Canada at the end of May 1985, opened his mouth wider than he should. He revealed that the Pentagon is devising a new war plan and command structure that would integrate offensive and defensive forces, army, navy, air and space commands – B-1s, Tridents, Pershing IIs, lasers and other ABM systems, cruise missiles, satellites and ASATs, and all the other hardware and software (including, presumably, air-breathing systems like Mr Heseltine) – into one single coordinated Command. All systems could then go in the twinkling of a Gigaflop.[77]

THE SOVIET RESPONSE TO SDI

In this compressed account of Europe's welcome to Star Wars the attentive reader may have noted that certain familiar characters have only had walk-on parts. First of all, the Soviet Union. It is of course predictable that True Believers in SDI, such as Lord Chalfont and the editor of *The Times*, should attribute all America's difficulties to 'the Soviet campaign against SDI' and to Soviet attempts to 'split the NATO alliance'. Of course, the Kremlin has looked on with fascination as NATO started falling about. But what has been the Soviet role?

The fact is that Soviet diplomacy in 1985 has been upstaged by the front-stage drama of the fratching among the NATO cousins. Any 'splits' in NATO have been wholly self-induced. All could have taken place as it did if the USSR had not existed, except as the Idea of the Other. Of course, Soviet publicists have turned up the volume control of propaganda against America's efforts to attain to first-strike superiority and its 'imperial ambition' to achieve world domination.[78] Perhaps they have a point. But the world has not really been listening.

It is true – as Lord Chalfont and others keep saying – that there is an element of hypocrisy in Soviet propaganda. The Soviet Union has never proposed to build its own SDI or impermeable shield, and it does not now. But as John Pike has shown, it has its own advanced piecemeal ABM researches, ASAT programme and the rest. The Russians also have more developed anti-aircraft and surface-to-air (SAM) defences than NATO, since a far greater proportion of United States offensive systems are air- or sea-based (27 per cent and 51 per cent) whereas most of Soviet warheads are based on land (65 per cent). The hypocrisy of Soviet publicists consists in their habitual secrecy about any of these developments and their pretence of Simon Pure innocence. In 1984 a Committee of Soviet Scientists for Peace against Nuclear Threat published an expert critique of SDI, which was derived entirely from unclassified US sources. It gives not one iota of information away about Soviet researches, despite the fact that its members included the Director and Deputy Director of the Institute of Space Research of the USSR Academy of Sciences.

Thus the Soviet military may well have nasty surprises of their own up their sleeves, and any treaties must be carefully drawn and verified. (Since there is as yet scarcely any independent citizen lobby in the Soviet Union capable of watching its own military – and what little there is, such as the Moscow Trust Group, is exposed to continual harassment from the KGB – American arms controllers and the Freeze movement are right to ask about verification.) Yet it is difficult to see any alternative to the Soviet diplomatic posture on SDI. They have proposed new treaties to outlaw all military developments in space, including ASAT systems. They have defended existing ABM and SALT treaties. Although treaties prohibiting research might be difficult to verify, as soon as research reaches the stage of testing or deployment verification should present few problems; if NORAD can 'track a glove' in space (p. 16), it can certainly track satellites, space mines or laser platforms. Above all, they have asked the USA to give up SDI, as a precondition of any progress in the Geneva arms talks.

Predictably this has met with outrage among the Reaganauts. The Soviet Union is blocking the Geneva talks and is trying to 'exploit' the divisions in NATO. Even the International Institute of Strategic Studies, whose annual survey criticizes SDI, says that 'the United States cannot reasonably be expected to make unilateral concessions' in abandoning SDI at Geneva. What does the Institute mean? Star Wars was imposed unilaterally, and without even consulting allies. Throughout the Euromissile crisis, apologists for Pershing II and cruise (who included the Institute) argued that these were necessary 'bargaining chips' in negotiations with the Soviet Union. Yet when these negotiations recommenced, the USA unilaterally raised the ante. Star Wars was 'non-negotiable', and the American negotiators refused to link the question of space and terrestrial systems. Is it probable that the Soviet military (who are as True Believers in MAD as their Western opposites) will agree to negotiate reducing the number of their missiles at the moment when the American military are advertising devices to shoot the remaining ones down?

We have seen that the most probable military response to ABM defences will be to multiply both warheads and penetration aids (p. 41). The USA is already working on this and the French are already planning, in response to possible Soviet ABM developments, to expand their *force de frappe* by the mid-1990s, from 98 warheads to 594, with accompanying decoys.[79] The British Trident will also be 'adapted' to 'overcome any Russian star-wars defence',[80] although on past form neither the British public nor Parliament will be told about it. The Soviet military have promised to do just the same.[81] 'As a practical matter,' said General Brent Scowcroft, who headed the President's Commission on Strategic Forces during Reagan's first term,

> It would be very difficult to induce the Soviets to reduce their offensive forces if they faced the prospect of a strategic defence for which they might need those forces to penetrate.[82]

Or as Professor Marshall Shulman, an expert on Soviet affairs, has written:

> By no conceivable logic can we expect the Russians to agree to reduce their offensive missiles while we are moving to gain military control of space, in addition to new bombers, missiles and submarines . . . under a nearly doubled military budget.[83]

The Soviet authorities no doubt wish to bury Star Wars, but their propaganda has been less strident than usual. Perhaps they do not wish to panic the European critics? They would prefer to attend as unobtrusive mourners at the funeral, and let President Mitterrand and Sir Geoffrey Howe carry the coffin. They have even sent constructive notes of inquiry as to the health of the sufferer. Mr Gorbachov has insisted that the matter remains negotiable. He by no means insists upon a 'unilateral' abandonment of SDI: he would happily negotiate a mutual deep cut in ICBMs in exchange.[84] More recently, there have been Soviet feelers to suggest that the ABM Treaty could be revised to permit 'research only' developments, or to permit ground-based (but not space-based) defensive systems to be introduced by mutual agreement alongside serious cuts in offensive systems on both sides.[85] Such proposals would be welcomed by the genuine arms controllers both in Congress and in West European establishments. They would restore the tranquillity of MAD.

The other familiar characters absent from this account have been the peace movements of Western Europe and (with the notable exception of the expert scientific and arms-control lobbies) of the United States. There have been no demonstrations of hundreds of thousands against Star Wars, and rather little activity of any kind. This may not be because the peace movements have joined with Colonel Alford's 'Europeans' in 'liking' nuclear weapons. Perhaps (as Professor Lawrence Freedman explained to *The New York Times*) it is because of the 'sheer exhaustion' of the activists?[86] The peace movements and the political forces closest to them have, of course, been against Star Wars, and mostly for the right reasons: it would carry the arms race into space, be destabilizing and destroy arms control, and it is a quest for American superiority. European socialist parties (including the British Labour Party) have taken the same wholesome stance; there has even been a *rapprochement* between the French Socialists and the German SPD (so bitterly divided over Pershing II) with a common statement against SDI.[87] The West German Greens have extended their opposition to the anti-human technologies of Eureka.

But this has mostly been a matter of position papers and press conferences. There has been little urgency and as much confusion as conviction. It is not easy to sit down against Star Wars. And if one marches with banners upon Downing Street one may encounter Sir Geoffrey Howe marching along to join the demo. The peace movement does not like that kind of thing at all. The intense encounters of 1981–3 have left all of us (opponents and apologists for Euromissiles) with emotional wounds and with a taste for resuming domestic confrontations along familiar political lines. The antagonists of yesteryear do not wish to be reconciled. Who is going to follow a banner carried by Professor Freedman and Professor Michael Howard?

In this the peace movement may have shown some wisdom. That banner was inscribed 'DEFEND MAD', which could not be the peace movement's cause. The activists preferred to stand on the pavements in amazement, watching their former opponents falling out among themselves. Yet in their failure to insert their own voices into the argument they may have been unwise. For the unexpected quietness of the European anti-nuclear movements has allowed the establishment to manage the discussion in its own way. A 'senior administration official' in Washington has noted with relief that 'the foreign ministries, the professional diplomats in most of these countries are running the show'. And 'a senior European diplomat' concurred:

> We can live with this situation for a while. There is no political pressure on this issue as there was regarding the deployment of the medium-range American missiles two years ago.[88]

'Running the show' has meant, in Britain, true to form, denying parliamentary time to debate the issue, so that the matter may be decided and the agreement be put in the post before people find out. It also means that the debate has scarcely been disclosed to viewers or to readers in the major media. The majority of the British people go about their business unaware that Folly's Comet is now overhead. And even some of those in the action-directed grassroots peace movements, who consider too much reading or even thinking to be 'elitist', have been too busy to look up at the stars. In this they may be mistaken. For the stars predict a future more earth-destroying than could even come from cruise.

MILITARY INTERESTS AND SDI

It is time to take some overview of Star Wars and to come to a conclusion. The project itself – an impermeable shield – is now generally accepted as impossible. Yet, in the name of this fantasy, political and economic forces are being mobilized which bring mankind within a new order of hazard. How are we to explain these seeming absurdities?

We cannot simply attribute all to the whims of President Reagan. Nations do not normally lay heavy burdens upon their taxpayers and inflate the national deficit just to humour the fantasies of a leader – even one just born-again from the ballot-box. Nor do entrenched establishments endanger their relations with their allies in pursuit of a strategic hypothesis.

There must be some hidden agenda here and some very powerful interests at work. It will be convenient to divide the motivating energies of Star Wars into three components, each of which complements and influences the other. These are military, industrial and ideological.

The military interests at work have been at the centre of this book. President Reagan did not invent SDI out of the air. He gathered together a number of ongoing military programmes (BMD, ASAT, laser research, etc.), tied them into a bundle and gave to them a new forward projection and a moral apologia. The military went along with the plan but tried to turn it to their own more specialized interests: silo defences, the abrogation of treaty limits, injections of dollars for their pet projects. The terms of SDI are generous enough – and vague enough – to hold out promise for everyone; there is little need, as yet, for inter-service competition. Nor are the offensive systems of the previous programmes being starved of funds. On the contrary, all are going forward together.

Where is this likely to lead? One thing only is certain – it will not lead to Reagan's utopia. History is a record of human intentions which are diverted to unintended conclusions. No leader's intentions, and no designs for the future, have ever survived the attrition of decades and emerged in the same form. If many billions of dollars are poured into Star Wars research, then *something* will result.

The most unlikely consequence would be that the pop-ups and the orbiting laser platforms would actually get into space. But if they should, then William E. Borrows, director of the Science and Environmental Reporting Programme at New York University, has suggested where that might end:

American fighting mirrors, laser battle stations, space planes and manned-attack platforms will sooner or later co-inhabit the heavens with their Soviet counterparts. Orbiting lasers made in California will be closely followed by space mines made in Yaroslav ... It will therefore be deemed imperative to develop weapons that can attack the mines before they attack the lasers that are supposed to attack the ICBMs that are launched to attack the cities and the silos ... The earth itself will have been turned into a gigantic orbiting bomb.[89]

What is certain is that the direction of the programme would progressively militarize science; would license heavier security controls over scientific, industrial and academic life; and would transfer military decisions to the programmed circuits of advanced computers. Many forward-looking thinkers would feel safer if the destiny of the earth was entrusted to a Gigaflop rather than to President Reagan, but traditionalists like Sir Geoffrey Howe are not among them. He is still old-fashioned enough to complain at 'a situation where the peace of the world rested solely upon computers and automatic decision-making'. For, as Lord Zuckerman has noted,

What is critically important is that there could be no human 'interface' in any part of the system. There would be no time for human judgement, no time for 'no-go' decisions. Once the surveillance satellites had registered a launching, the system would be automatically triggered to execute its single option – to destroy.[90]

The projections of Mr Borrows and Lord Zuckerman are every bit as valid as the projections of SDI. But neither are likely to come about. The fact is that the military *don't know* what their more exotic researches will lead to. How could they? What they want is the money to find out, and they are happy to let the President front for this by telling the world a moral story. Some of the experiments and projects they are into are weird and wonderful. Some are working on anti-matter, and are confident that 'anti-matter beams could provide an effective and highly lethal kill mechanism'.[91] Mr Peres, the Prime Minister of Israel, after emissaries from Washington had persuaded him to come in on SDI, said that he was shown proposals to set up an American missile factory on the moon: 'I know that this sounds far-fetched, but it appears as a real and near-at-hand possibility from the material I've read.'[92] The chief scientist for SDI, Gerold Yonas, is interested in the 'Jedi Concept', for 'firing globs of plasma (a cloud of highly energized atomic nuclei and electrons) at nearly the speed of light'.[93]

No one knows where research in the name of Star Wars may lead, but a few people may know more than others. An executive at the Livermore Laboratory hinted darkly to a *Newsweek* reporter that 'the things most discussed in public are the ones the government is least interested in'.[94] The American system has real virtues of openness, and it is immeasurably more open than the Russian. Persons of con-science and whistle-blowers have informed the public in ways which (at least until Clive Ponting's trial) would have been inconceivable in Britain. Yet the very openness of a part of the system may distract attention from other parts which are deeply classified. One recalls how for twenty years all military developments in space were classified under the rhetoric of 'space for peace' (p. 14). Star Wars may be the same disguise – for example, for the advanced development of space-to-earth weapons, the 'orbiting bomb' returned in a new form. As Senator Larry Pressler has noted, SDI 'is probably going to be an offensive-weapons system':

Anything that can destroy a foreign ICBM within seconds after it is launched would also be capable of delivering a weapon in the same area.[95]

Space-based death rays, it has been suggested, might be 'torched' to burn out grain fields, oil-storage tanks and other targets, and 'take an industrialized country back to an eighteenth-century level in thirty minutes'. The first nation to send up space-based lasers of this power would have 'the longest "big stick" in history' and 'the capability for unilateral control of outer space and consequent domination of the earth'.[96]

If such 'kill mechanisms' are on the way, we will not be told. And the neat new weapons, while suitable for space, might perform even more nicely on earth. Not only the Americans, but also the Russians – or the Japanese or Germans or British – are likely to make additions to the inventory of 'lethality'.

Seen in this way the military interests are secondary partners in Star Wars. They do not motivate the programme but they have crowded behind the banner of SDI and are rushing it forward in pursuit of a multitude of longstanding strategic and service interests. Their research interests combine perfectly with the second component which is an authentic motivating force driving Star Wars forward: the rapacity of the 'military–industrial–academic' complex.

THE GIANT ARMS CONTRACTORS

We have seen (Chapter 1) that Star Wars was conceived by those whom Lord Zuckerman once called 'the alchemists of the laboratories' – the R & D lobby in the high-tech and aerospace industries. As soon as the President gave to it his favour, very powerful interests have mobilized behind it. As Hans A. Bethe and his fellow scientists have warned, SDI is acquiring 'institutional momentum'. 'When a trillion dollars is waved at the US aerospace industry, the project will rapidly acquire a life of its own – independent of its public justification'; it will become an unstoppable 'juggernaut'.[97]

Projections of the cost of deploying SDI range from $400 billion to $1 trillion and above. Even projections of the cost of research over the coming five years – usually given as $26 billion – fluctuate, not only because these are subject to annual congressional modification, but also because SDI budgetary estimates do not include a number of research projects (ASAT, radar, Department of Energy) already ongoing before SDI, which will continue simultaneously. Taking these into account, research and testing of SDI components might cost some $90 billion between 1984 and 1994, at which time a decision would be taken on initial deployments.[98] It has been estimated that between 1984 and 1990 SDI projects will move up from 3.7 per cent to 15.7 per cent of the Defense Department's R & D budget.[99] According to figures provided by the independent Center on Budget and Policy Priorities, by 1987 the SDI research budget will have overtaken the budget for deployment of the MX or the Midgetman missiles or for Trident II. Star Wars will then be at the leading edge of the military–industrial complex.

Even this is not the whole story. Countering criticisms that SDI could be easily evaded by underflying aircraft and cruise missiles, Weinberger advised that the shield must be supplemented by an additional programme of air and coastal defences (radar, interceptor aircraft and SAMs) at a cost of $50 billion a year.[100] (This may perhaps explain the suggestion that NATO allies should subcontract into a 'TDI', and pick up some of the costs of research and development.) And we must add to this, in the looking-glass world of 'deterrence', the anti-Star-Wars programme of penetration aids and foxy tricks which is already being funded.

We do not have to speculate upon who is behind all this, since they can be identified. Eighty-seven per cent of the SDI and ASAT contracts of financial years 1983 and 1984 were received by ten contractors. Eight of these ten were among the Pentagon's Top Twenty private arms contractors. They included the major contractors building offensive weapons: the MX (Rockwell, TRW, AVCO), the B-1 bomber (Rockwell, AVCO, Boeing, LTV), Trident (Lockheed) and cruise missiles (Boeing, Litton). The others in the top ten were McDonnell Douglas, Hughes Aerospace and Teledyne. Martin Marietta (the contractors for Pershing II) came in in thirteenth place, after Ford Aerospace and Science Applications International Corporation. No doubt the table seating will change as other giants move up, like Grumman, General Electric and Honeywell, and as new high-tech consortiums are set up. But this is where the thrust comes from.[101]

Two other interesting points arise from these early contracts. First, 72 per cent of the large long-term contracts so far have gone to US Army projects related to terminal ABM defences: i.e. point defence.[102]

And in 1983 and 1984 45 per cent of space-weapons prime contracts went to the President's home state, California. Moreover, 77 per cent of the prime contracts went to states or districts represented by Congresspersons or Senators who sit on the armed services committees and the defence appropriations subcommittees.[103] That is how the pork barrel works.

The workings of this lobby are transparent and are legitimated by free-market ideology. (In fact, the notion that such contracting is competitive is largely a spoof: the giants negotiate with the Pentagon and each other, and the major contracts are not put out to open tender.) In a sense, the world's peace movements must take a share of the blame for these developments. They had made nukes unpopular and the giant weapons contractors could see the future market for endless 'modernizations' and 'new generations' of offensive weapons beginning to shrink. Their shareholders felt insecure.

Military research requires long lead times (of five, ten, or more years) and in less than five years the order-books for MX, Midgetman, Pershing II, the B-1, and for some cruise missiles would be empty. What on earth could the hapless giants do then? Answer: they must go into space, and pretend it was for 'defence'. SDI research contracts are simply the seed money for developing the next generation of orders. Meanwhile the giants will be kept alive by pushing their existing stock. But they want to be sure that the seed will grow into a new crop. As one contractor said: 'Everybody knows that you don't make money on technology research programmes. We've got to have deployment.' Or as Boeing's representative added, 'There is an awful lot of money here ... If we can do something for the government that is within our resources and make money, we will. We are not philanthropic.'[104]

These giants subcontract much work to the minnows of the trade, and to computer and electronics companies (some of whom hope to grow into whales). And by 1985 there was a stampede of smaller projectors to the doors of General Abrahamson's SDIO. An investment analyst published a newsletter calling SDI 'money from Heaven', and another commentator likened the excitement among high-tech operators to 'a fish-feeding frenzy'. The scientists already in the weapons laboratories were enlisted to enlarge the military–industrial–academic complex. Some universities were pushovers. The universities of Alabama, Arizona and South Florida received early contracts; Carnegie-Mellon at Pittsburgh won (against stiff competition) a $100 million contract as home for the Air Force's Software Engineering Institute; the State University of New York at Buffalo formed a 'consortium' with GEC and the Naval Research Laboratory for SDI researches, with $2.5 million budgeted for the next three years.[105]

But to their credit both scientists and administrators at leading universities have refused to be seduced. A critical objection, in the United States as in Europe, is the Pentagon's insistence that 'principal investigators' should have security clearances, and the fear that research will become classified and withdrawn from publication. And American scholars, with their remarkable traditions of international exchange, are offended by recent government attempts to limit contacts with foreign colleagues (whether Communist or not). Money is winning the argument in the less reputable centres. The Georgia Institute of Technology has received a ninefold increase in Defense Department funds since 1976, perhaps because it 'takes few foreign students' and 'lets' its students receive security clearances, as 'just another union card'.[106]

Thus the complex which unites Boeing, NORAD, Georgia Tech and Livermore Laboratory is a powerful motivator of SDI. It expends millions on lobbying, its personnel inter-operate with the Pentagon (in the past three years 2,300 Pentagon staff have 'retired' straight into jobs with the arms contractors),[107] and it has placed tame representatives as salesmen on key congressional committees. It supplies not only the material sinews of Star Wars but also some of its ideology. Rockwell International (contractors for the MX and the B-1 bomber) has long had a Space-operations and Satellite-systems Department, and its director said in 1981:

Rockwell, obviously, has been spending some time over the years thinking about – hopefully on a bipartisan basis – what the US space programme should be.

It also has a Space-transportation System Development Department, which contracts for the space shuttle. It has (in competition with Boeing) been developing a Space-operations Centre – an orbiting eight-person space station. It also has ideas for 'an on-demand launch vehicle, to get anywhere on earth within ninety minutes', and, in the twenty-first century, a geostationary space base, 22,250 miles up, hovering above the globe: the ultimate military command post, with 'global battle-management capability'.

Rockwell and its cousins do not just wait for demand and then research to supply. They supply to politicians and the public the ideological and military demand which then they supply once more with weapons. Colonel Morgan W. Sanborn, USAF (retired), manager of new business requirements for Rockwell's space-transportation section is an example of the breed of leg-men who move from the Pentagon to the contractors and who also act as PR men to the influential public. He also has a taste for global history: 'Past civilizations have risen and fallen and the West seems to be in decline . . . Space is an area where we might establish new goals, galvanize public opinion, regain our momentum.'[108]

This ideological rationale was projected by Rockwell in a booklet entitled *Space, America's Frontier for Growth, Leadership and Freedom*. It warned about America's decline in economic growth, dependence on imported fossil fuels, loss of military superiority and 'decline in national morale'. It reminds us that if the arms contractors are 'not philanthropists', at least they can wear philanthropy's mask. The mask that they have donned in the past year or two is that of their benevolent mission to the whole national economy. The space programme is 'at the very frontier of technology' and it 'spawns technological advancements that ultimately help to foster higher productivity, open new markets, and develop new products'. The SDI research will have amazing spin-offs which will carry the whole US economy into a third industrial revolution.

This corresponds very closely to the analysis proposed by M. Cheysson (p. 119) – that the true motivation of Star Wars is not military at all. It is to enhance the competitiveness of US capitalism, through measures of 'military Keynesianism'. This has some force, yet it may be over-logical. The messy interests involved do not suggest a prescient governing rationale. And the difficulties should be considered.

Powerful as these lobbies are, yet they are not majority shareholders in the US economy. Insofar as they grasp resources, they will compete with the resources of other sectors: farming, construction, transportation, manufacturing, the service industries, health, education and the rest. In any budget retrenchment, SDI will even compete with other, more credible, demands of the armed services. It will also compete for personnel and skills; already more than one in eight of America's scientists and engineers are working on 'defence' retainers.

Moreover, the diversion of vast resources towards non-consumable ends – throwing billions of dollars into holes in space – with a steadily rising federal budget deficit, might be the way to destroy the US economy and to weaken its competitive power. Many experts directly contradict the euphoric promises of civil spin-off from Star Wars research. While there are some examples of such spin-off in the past, Japanese and West German developments in computers, micro-processors and high-tech have been attributed to the fact that these nations spend *less* on military R & D than the United States and Britain, and correspondingly more on civilian research.[109] And military development is turning increasingly towards what Mary Kaldor has called 'baroque' products – obscenely ornate, technologically fragile and expensive dead-end products, with no possible civil relevance. What possible civil organization could require a seventh-generation computer performing at thirty Gigaflops a second – unless perhaps the police?[110]

It has been one of the dreams of the Star Warriors that they might incite the Soviet Union into a 'technological end-run', a competition in space so expensive that it would bring down the Soviet economy in ruins. Dr Edward Teller favours this prospect. Star Wars would have 'a devastating impact' on the Soviet economy and defence establish-ment: 'Forcing them to reduce the burn phase will obsolete all their weapons and force them into very costly expenditures.'[111] The noted strategic space expert, Dr Isaac Asimov, has added:

> I don't think Star Wars is feasible and I don't think anyone takes it seriously. It's just a device to make the Russians go broke. But we'll go broke too. It's very much of a John Wayne standoff.

Undoubtedly the cost of SDI experiments, at a time when they are trying to revive their own flagging economy, is one reason why Soviet leaders so much dislike the venture. But it is a practical question whose economy will break first. Will Star Wars fall into the hole being dug by the US deficit? Will we look back on the whole episode as a kind of South Sea Bubble, a psychodrama in which corrupt politicians, cynical speculators and the gullible public collapsed the economy in debt?

The SDI spin-off is more likely to be 'a drip-off'.[112] It may even come to be seen by the American public as a rip-off. Huge sectors of private industry will get no cut at the cake. At the same time as appropriations for SDI are being forced through, federal funding for welfare, health or farming are being cut or stopped outright: child nutrition, urban and rural development, the 'Job Corps'. Resentment is growing at the bribery, guaranteed high profit levels, costing and general inefficiency endemic to the weapons industry.[113] The areas of industrial decline in the north-east and the mid west resent their federal taxes being channelled to the arms contractors of the prosperous southern rim. If the American public should detect that SDI is not about a shield at all but is likely to enhance the dangers of nuclear war, then the Freeze movement might swiftly be reborn, but in a tougher form, in which the anger of the ripped-off American poor united with the altruism of the peace campaigners. The military–bureaucratic– industrial–academic complex is immensely powerful. But it is not all of America, nor all of America's industry and academies. It does not have to win.

THE IDEOLOGY OF NUCLEAR ISOLATIONISM

For this reason the instincts of the ailing incumbent of the White House may have been more realistic than the advice of his pushy aides. He is still stubbornly defending Star Wars Mark I. If his aides think Star Wars Mark II can be better marketed in Europe, that's all right. But he doesn't want the American people to know. It is Star Wars I – the technological epiphany – which is keeping America quiet and the Freeze movement down.

And this is the third, and perhaps the dominant, motivating force behind Star Wars. The project has an independent life within American ideology. The vision is held most strongly by the President himself. He is himself no kind of strategist and he could not tell MAD from NUTS. What he is is a superbly successful populist politician who can tune a policy like a precision missile and home it in on to the prejudices of Middle America.

In its ideological expression Star Wars is the ultimate decomposition of deterrence theory, and the attempt by US nuclear ideologists to return to the womb of Hiroshima. Ever since the USSR reached forward to nuclear 'parity' they have become increasingly fretful. They possessed this huge bludgeoning and blackmailing power – which, however, could never be used, and the world was beginning to tumble to the fact.

For a decade this giant, the US military, has been locked like a wrestler in the nuclear arms of its Soviet opposite in a struggle to gain superiority, but neither has been successful. Then the ideologists tried out menus of fine-tuned options and scenarios of 'limited' nuclear war on the territory of their allies or of other nations. These have proved to be implausible, and have even been met with ingratitude.

Delving back in their memories, President Reagan and his friends recalled those blissful years, from 1945 to 1950, when the United States had the Bomb and the Other did not. It is out of that regression to an idealized golden sanctuary in the past that the ideological and political drive of Star Wars has come. Let us abolish the Other's Bomb! Let us arm the moral ends of the USA with an impermeable shield! Let us once again be able to threaten a world which cannot retaliate on us!

As one hawkish armchair strategist, Colin Gray, has written:

In the event that the United States succeeded in deploying a population defence that was technically robust, a considerable measure of US freedom of political action should be restored as a logical consequence.[114]

(This might also restore a 'freedom' to conduct conventional wars.) As Caspar Weinberger told the Senate Armed Services Committee in 1984:

If we can get a system which is effective and which we know can render their weapons impotent, we could be back in a situation we were in, for example, when we were the only nation with a nuclear weapon.[115]

Once this solution was found (out of pure ideology), then money and knowhow *must* be able to bring it about. And Star Wars is a populist's dream. It is the Rococo Epiphany, the ultimate technological fix, the all-singing-all-dancing-all-praying-all-answering machine. It has struck a gusher of American rhetoric in whose fountains there float and jostle incompatible elements. Like much in the history of American populism it appeals at one and the same time to the democratic and the authoritarian, to innocence and to 'know-nothing' self-interest, to the generous and to the mean instincts of the American people. It evokes a nostalgic golden past Before the Bomb (or before the machine got into the garden) at the same time as it appeals to generations brought up on sci-fi, on space invaders, on Darth Vader and Luke Skywalker movies, and on their own home-terminal computer games. It massages the

American ego by intoning homilies about 'destroying missiles, not lives' while drawing humanity within new dimensions of danger.

More than this, in a match of astonishing simplicity it combines isolationism (they can't get us) with external braggadocio and menace – if they can't get at us, then 'robust anti-Communism can be adopted at the verbal and conventional level without giving everyone the shud-ders'.[116] It comes even, to a generation long exercising its imagination on scenarios of space, with a sense of inevitability. And it is as American as apple-pie. It combines the citizen's faith that whatever the US of A does must be moral – and that the Bomb is God's gift to protect the 'Free World' – with the energetic and innovative American tradition of 'fixing' things, and of looking for technological solutions to political, social or even psychological problems. With its groovy furniture of lasers and rail-guns, and its vocabulary of 'megavolts and terrawatts and gigajoules', it exudes the vibes of a New World going places once again. It is a kid's dream, which Pa still remembers as he plays with his pocket computer. And polls suggest that far more men buy it than women. Technology is a surrogate macho.[117]

Star Wars, with its futurist glitter, encodes ideological forces which act in their own right. We should not dismiss it as mere rhetorical sham. The President himself may be a true believer. And one of the elements encoded is one in which he has long been a specialist – in evoking a sense of American insecurity before the 'Communist threat'. Anti-Communism (and before that anti-Socialism or anti-Anarchism) has always been a central strand in the American populist Right, in binding together all the heterogeneous ethnic elements which make up the American people and giving them a sense of nationhood against the threat of the Other. If Americans were distracted from 'standing up to the Commies' then they might take more notice of how they were being ripped off at home. But the genius of Star Wars is to offer a tech-nological defence which requires no political resolution, no modifi-cation of ideological posture – in fact, no political exercise at all. The Star Warriors can turn their backs on détente, they can give up on international relations, they can (if they wish) opt out of the United Nations. The Threat will still be there (to be stirred up in American culture whenever needed) but the missiles of the 'evil empire' will be kept out. It is for these reasons that the extreme protagonists of the Right, both old and new, both in the USA and in Europe, have given it their support. Senator Jesse Helms and Dr Jerry Falwell of the

Moral Majority have joined the board of American Space Frontiers, which is raising money from 'retired people and housewives in the sunbelt states' to intervene against critics of SDI in congressional elections.[118]

This eschatological zeal has long been found in the traditions of American populism. Did not Theodore Roosevelt campaign in the elections of 1912 behind the song: 'We stand at Armageddon and we battle for the Lord'? To find the most powerful nation on earth to be regressing into an ideological second childhood is a sign that an epoch is coming to an end. It is a terrifying signal of our predicament. The combination of material avarice (the arms lobby), military pursuit of whatever they can get, and of ideological self-delusion may prove to be the terminal dementia of the nuclear age.

There is no technological fix for the fraught and complex political relations between nations. There will never be an impermeable shield against nuclear evil. There is – and there has been for forty years – only one shield against chaos: that pitifully weak and yet somehow indestructible shield, the human conscience. It is as full of holes as a sieve, but it has kept chaos out for forty years. It is time to put it in repair.

CONCLUSIONS AND POSTSCRIPT

The *Economist* has announced (August 1985) its conversion to Star Wars. The reason (it speculates) for most people's 'contemptuous dismissal' of SDI was simply that 'most people usually find new ideas incredible'. But, also, the President's Star Wars I 'is now generally admitted to be wildly implausible'. The *Economist*'s conversion is, of course, to Star Wars II, and it is relieved that 'the Reaganites – well, most of them – have come clean about what they have in mind'. Mark II is a 'silos-and-headquarters-protecting screen', 'capable of stopping quite a lot of the Soviet warheads aimed at America's nuclear forces and command centres'. This is commended, as improving the strength of the American nuclear umbrella over herself and over Europe/Japan. It is also commended as an 'anti-nuclear idea', which causes embarrassment to the anti-nuclear movement. If the Russians should eventually get an SDI too, then – at a further eventuality – the superpowers might agree on cutting down their nuclear armouries.[119]

This perhaps indicates the way in which some heads in the British establishment are now turning. It is not easy to decide whether these arguments arise from cynicism or levity. Any historian of ideas could tell the *Economist* that 'new ideas' beneficial to humankind have not normally been announced by politicians and then instantly been supported by the armed forces and by industrialists and incarnated in budgetary appropriations. It is more usual for new ideas to survive on bread-and-cheese on the margins of respectable society for several decades before they are noticed by the editors of reputable weeklies. Nor is it clear how a strategy which, the *Economist* concedes, is designed to improve a nuclear umbrella and to protect the nuclear missile silos of one party is 'an anti-nuclear idea'.

The editor of the *Economist* knows no more than any of us what in fact the researches of Star Wars will produce, what deathly cultures may be forced into life within the hothouse of those billions of dollars. He should know better than most the extraordinary and unpredictable outcomes of research and development. He must know that priority is being given to directed-energy beams with high 'kill mechanisms' and the like. He could deduce that, whatever new strategy evolves from this, a great deal of high-tech military shit will result, and some of it will be lofted into space. One is dismayed by the frailty of the human intellect, and the levity with which those who form opinions fall in behind each new folly. For if, with chic self-interest, we assent to the easy choice today, how can we know what foul options we will pass on to successor generations? We have no right to pass on enhanced technologies of murder to the unknown politicians of the twenty-first century, who may turn out to be even crazier than the lot we have now.

Star Wars is in no way 'an anti-nuclear idea'. We prefer the definition offered by the distinguished strategic theorist, Mr Caesar Voute:

Star Wars is the product of a bunch of people with the political sophistication of starving crocodiles, who will not stop until every can of worms has been opened.[120]

These are our conclusions:

1. Star Wars, both I and II, offer to zap (all or some) incoming missiles. Research and deployment will take two or three decades, at astronomic cost. Exactly the same objective could be achieved, with an immediate saving of cost, by nuclear disarmament. If total mutual disarmament (Star Wars I) is beyond this century's reach, partial

disarmament ('stopping quite a lot' of warheads), which is the aim of Star Wars II, could commence tomorrow.

2. If Star Wars has not yet shown that it can stop any missiles, yet it does have one achievement to its account. Throughout 1985 it stopped dead the Geneva arms talks. It appears likely, at the time that this book goes to press, to prevent any progress from being made at the Reagan–Gorbachov summit.

The activity of millions over the past years, the initiatives of non-aligned nations, the pleas of the world's professional and religious bodies – all this goodwill is being squandered, and the hopes of all are being defrauded – simply because President Reagan and his closest advisers have upped the ante with SDI, and then insisted that this chip is 'non-negotiable'. And to emphasize the obduracy of their position they have disregarded Soviet gestures (the moratorium on nuclear testing and ASAT tests) and ostentatiously continued with their own programmes. Indeed, so anxious were they to test the US second-generation ASAT before the summit that they shot down one of their own working satellites, which was still providing scientific data, out of the sky.[121]

Despite the obduracy of President Reagan and his immediate circle, there is clearly a sharp argument within the United States administration, and also between the USA and her NATO allies. If Reagan should decide, after all, that SDI is negotiable, then how might negotiations unroll? Some kites are being flown (in both Washington and Moscow) which suggest the following resolution: there will be deep cuts (of perhaps 50 per cent) in ICBMs by both superpowers, and at the same time the ABM Treaty might be 'revised' to permit a certain level of missile-silo BMD defences on both sides. Such defences might initially be ground-based – that is, ground-to-air anti-missile missiles, with few space-based components. Perhaps the Soviet military might accept this trade-off, since, as John Pike has shown, this is the area in which their own BMD preparations are already most advanced. According to this compromise, the ABM Treaty would not then be abrogated but would be redrawn by mutual agreement.

At first sight this might appear to be a positive compromise. The large reduction in weapons on both sides would have at least symbolic hopefulness, and it might signal a reduction in tension between the superpowers in which political resolutions might be fostered. BMD terminal defences of the remaining missile silos might be seen only as a form of 'hardening' their survivability and capacity for retaliatory attack: that is, the reinforcement of the rule of MAD. It would also reinforce the bipolar rule of the superpowers, and signify a deal over the rest of the world's heads.

Yet how far would this really advance the prospects of peace? There are two important reservations to be made. First, deep cuts in the heavy stuff – the ICBMs – need in no way limit the qualitative modernization of the new weaponry (like Trident D-5) coming along. As Gorbachov himself has pointed out, the 'most dangerous area' of the nuclear arms race is that 'of qualitative improvement'.[122] This 'improvement' is now going ahead fast, not only in ICBMs but in short- and inter-mediate-range weapons, in submarine- and air-launched missiles (especially cruise), and even in nuclear artillery. Mr Denis Healey is quite right to argue that as important – if not *more* important – than cuts in the old obsolescent stock, is 'a freeze on the development and deployment of new nuclear weapons', accompanied by a comprehensive ban on all nuclear tests (*Observer*, 29 September 1985).

Second, if the superpowers agree to limited BMD defences for their missile silos, this must not serve as an excuse for the development and testing of new exotic technologies. For any revision of the ABM Treaty could legitimate immense forward budgets 'just for research'. Since Mrs Thatcher, Chancellor Kohl and others have approved of SDI, but for 'research only', it is necessary to be clear that this is a very difficult line to draw. Mr Gorbachov tried to define this line in his interview with *Time* magazine. He did not propose a ban on 'research in fundamental science':

Such research concerning space is going on and it will continue. What we mean is the designing stage, when certain orders are given, contracts are signed, for specific elements of the systems. And when they start building models or mock-ups or test samples, when they hold field tests . . .

But research at the level of funding already in the Star Wars pipeline must lead on to models and prototypes, and test simulation will be no alternative to the real article. Already Pentagon sources are saying that 'near-term' testing of SDI components is imminent. 'Research only' would break through the ABM Treaty before 1990. In any case, if billions of dollars are poured into research, this will generate an 'unstoppable momentum' (as Sir Geoffrey Howe has warned) for deployment. The giant contractors will demand to plough all that seedcorn into a profitable harvest.

There is also another act to watch. An arms-control agreement is an agreement between the superpowers. At the same time as 'controlling' arms, they enter into collusion to control the world by agreement, and to control their own allies. An agreement advantageous to them may increase the dependent status of the rest of the world.

There have been curious moments when, in the midst of seeming antagonism, the arms controllers and nuclear scientists of the USA and the USSR have come to share a common interest in 'deterrence' and in ongoing research: 'They feel friendly and hand-picked – almost mystically picked. There's a sense of camaraderie.' Such camaraderie between Soviet and American nuclear scientists is held to have led to their common opposition in the late 1950s and early 1960s to a comprehensive test-ban treaty, which could have put them out of business.[123] No doubt such 'camaraderie' might defend laser and particle-beam researches today.

3. If Star Wars is offensive to Europeans, it is an obscenity to the peoples of the Third World. (Mr Rajiv Gandhi is said to have told the President this, to his face, when invited to a Cabinet meeting in June 1985, which almost caused a presidential apoplexy.) It has moved China to a more sharply worded non-aligned position, denouncing the militarization of space. No one has offered any shields to the Third World. A shield over one or both nuclear superpowers would only dramatize the vulnerability to threat of the non-nuclear developing nations and the failure of the former to observe the Non-Proliferation Treaty. The monstrous diversion of human resources into holes in space would mock the hunger of the world's poor. And the ulterior objectives of SDI (and Eureka) of maintaining technological superiority would add insult to injury.

4. Clearly, the best resolution of the whole question would be an American climb-down on Star Wars, accompanied by more stringent agreements (registered in the forum of the United Nations) prohibiting all further measures for the militarization of space and reducing existing military-related systems. We will not prescribe the optimum terms of possible treaties. We favour the observance of existing treaties (SALT, Outer Space, ABM and Non-Proliferation) and the withdrawal of existing ASAT systems. In addition, observation satellites

under independent auspices might provide for verification of existing treaties. We pass over the exact terms of this to more expert discussion.[124]

In the matter of arms-control measures, there may be a difference in emphasis between some American and West European opinion. Confronted by the SDI lobby and by imminent US breakout from treaties, American peace opinion is ardently defending the arms-control process. Our fellow-contributor, John Pike, is a notable member of this lobby.

We respect this position and support it. But in Europe, if we do not go beyond arms control, then we can find ourselves behind the banner: 'DEFEND MAD'. If Star Wars is a delirium which signals that an epoch is coming to an end, then let the epoch that is ending be that of 'deterrence'. For arms control negotiated between the two superpowers may simply be a way of regulating deterrence and keeping the rest of the world in place.

5. The British contributors can feel no satisfaction whatsoever in the role played by their own country in the events of 1985. New Zealand has provided an example to the world in refusing visits by nuclear-armed warships, and Australia has rejected the invitation to subcontract for SDI; Canada, which stands in a more sensitive relation both strategically and politically to the United States than does Britain, has after a full public and parliamentary discussion declined to enter any arrangement with SDI;[125] but the British government has shifted furtively from one foot to another, and done its best to limit all public and parliamentary discussion of an issue which affects the survival of the nation.

The official British have tried to ride, not two, but three or four horses. Sir Geoffrey Howe's commendable speech was poorly supported by fellow ministers. Mr Heseltine has hustled across to Washington, pleading the 'special relationship', and offering to sell British support for SDI provided that Britain got a $2 billion cut. He met with a humiliating brush-off.[126] Mrs Thatcher has become increasingly shrill, venting her wrath (as she often does when in difficulties) upon the French. French and British infighting for arms contracts has become more and more open, Mrs Thatcher appealing directly to President Reagan for his support for US army purchase of the Plessey–Rockwell-International Ptarmigan battlefield communications system (for some $4 billion) as against the tender of the French Thomson Csf. Mrs Thatcher pleaded the 'loyalty' of Britain to Star Wars, as against French perfidy, and (it seems) threatened that if Britain lost the contract, this loyalty might end.[127] Brushed off once again, Mrs Thatcher and Mr Heseltine soothed their foul tempers by signing a deal to modernize the Saudi Arabian air force.

When the issues before this nation are considered, this has been a pathetic and dishonourable exercise in furtive double-dealing. It has demonstrated 'loyalty' to no one, least of all to the British people.

6. One of the hidden agendas behind SDI becomes every day more clear. The US-based multinationals and giant arms contractors have revealed that they have no intention of sharing either SDI funding or technological exchanges with European competitors. The West Germans have been told, once again, that they are regarded as 'leaky', and can expect 'no two-way exchange' on Star Wars research.[128] Restrictions upon the use of even existing American hi-tech in Europe are being tightened. The Pentagon is now seeking to control the use of two 'supercomputers' at Manchester and London universities, and is provoking increasing resistance from among computer experts, scientists and trade unionists.[129]

This suggests that the needs of 'defence' are being used as a pretext to bring Western Europe directly within the technological and security controls of the multinationals. (The giant computer multinational, IBM, is a major shareholder in Rockwell International, and is said to exercise influence within the CIA.) The goal of this project is to integrate the 'Free World' within a single information-and-control system, at the same time as all military control is centralized in a single automated US command. It appears like a sci-fi nightmare, yet we know that this nightmare has visited the controllers of SDI. Gerold Yonas, chief scientist for SDIO, has written that 'the problem of integrating human behaviour and political institutions with rapidly evolving technology may prove to be the most difficult and crucial challenge to humanity's long-term survival'.[130] One notes that human beings are seen as subordinate to the technology with which they must be integrated.

We hope that this does, indeed, prove to be difficult. We mean to make it so.

✻

7. West European policies remain confused, with the West Germans and British trying to make private deals with the SDIO, with individual firms looking for subcontracts, and with the French still hoping to promote a manned European space-station from the matrix of the Ariane rocket (which has unkindly blown up in President Mitterrand's face).

In so far as Eureka indicates an impulse towards greater economic autonomy from the USA, which could hold open options for non-exploitative trading relations with the Soviet bloc and with developing nations, it can be supported. In so far as it is an idiot's copy of the technologies of SDI and has almost no social or environmental content, it cannot.

At present the military inflexions of European alternatives are becoming more evident. The proposed TDI (or Tactical Defence Initiative) has now been rechristened as EDI (or European Defence Initiative). At Bonn Chancellor Kohl's Christian Democratic Party is clamouring for the development of defences against Soviet cruise missiles, short-range missiles, and bombers—the stuff that will underfly a Star Wars 'shield'.[131]

Such developments may seem to be inevitable with each uprush in offensive capacities. The Soviet military are also developing their own defences against Pershing II and cruise missiles, as well as against cruise-launching bombers (B-52s) and submarines. Yet such defences will contribut to the security of neither side, not only because they will be leaky, but, even more, because this dangerous offensive-defensive mix will encourage the temptation to regard a nuclear war as being more fightable. This will only add another twist to folly's spiral.

8. What continues to astound us is the excitement generated by spurious technological fixes and the readiness with which parliaments find huge public funding for any type of provocative military hardware, compared with the indifference or hostility shown towards any attempt to find a political resolution of the antagonism between the blocs.

Star Wars and EDI pretend to stop (some of) the missiles when they are sent. The peace movements are trying to ensure political conditions in which no nation will want to send them and they will be progressively dismantled.

Washington and Whitehall warn that we must not allow the 'Soviet-inspired' campaign against SDI to split NATO and divide Europe from America. Yet the danger to world peace lies, precisely, in the unnatural bi-polar division of the world, with the resultant incitement to military and ideological hostility.

The real message of Star Wars to West Europe is to get out from under America's hegemony – and umbrella – as soon as we can. The obduracy of the United States about SDI should be the signal for a European Declaration of Independence, with independent, non-aligned diplomacies which would contribute to the security of both super-powers and of the world.

This is not the same as crossing over from the American to the Soviet "side". West Europe should now come forward as a mediator, developing trade, cultural and second-tier diplomatic relations with East European nations, while at the same time every kind of direct citizen's initiative to break through the ideological and security barriers between the blocs should be encouraged. Nations, East and West, should be brought into common agreements for mutual security (including nuclear-free zones and demilitarized zones of peace), with the objective of loosening the bloc structures of both sides, and healing the divisions between the two.

These constructive strategies have long been advanced by Europe's peace movements, and in particular by END (or European Nuclear Disarmament). They require, not futuristic hardware, but human intelligence and initiative, to which every citizen can contribute. The most painful technology may be to learn a language from the 'other side' and travel with a pack on one's back. The R & D for peaceful exploration of our own divided planet will cost one thousandth of the forward funding for SDI. Yet the governments of NATO and their agencies do all in their power to obstruct and to misrepresent the work of peace.

This takes us beyond the limits of this book, and we hesitate to venture even further, into space. Nor is it likely that the contributors would find a common position if (God forbid!) they were sent in a satellite aloft. The oldest contributor might say that humankind has found this globe a sufficient and not inhospitable dwelling-place since civilization began. And that we should learn to order human affairs better, and to care for the resources and environment of earth more wisely, before trespassing in space. Other contributors might note that the option is now closed for ever. And that, since the human imagination has already assaulted space, we should propose alternatives to Star Wars which reclaim the adventures of space for peace and for international cooperation. There are still some fragments of authentic cooperative scientific exploration in being (p. 48), there are some splendid proposals for future endeavours.[132] In a period of superpower reconciliation some great international space enterprise could express a sense of global community, and at a tithe of the cost of Star Wars.

But all of us would agree that the vision of peaceful space has, in the past twenty years, been utterly polluted. The heavens have lost their innocence, and what was once the seat of the deities now 'wears man's smudge and shares man's smell'.[133] If we are to restore the innocence to space, then we must learn to smell better on earth.

We would do well to remember that one of the earliest recorded voyages of an astronaut is that of Milton's Satan, who stumbled in space upon the dominion of Chaos:

> . . . in sudden view appear
> The secrets of the hoarie deep, a dark
> Illimitable Ocean without bound,
> Without dimension, where length, breadth, and highth,
> And time and place are lost; where eldest Night
> And *Chaos*, Ancestors of Nature, hold
> Eternal *Anarchie*, amidst the noise
> Of endless warrs, and by confusion stand.

And we might also remember the sin by which Satan and his angels fell.

Folly's Comet has a political and ideological, as well as military, nucleus. Astronomers classify comets, not as celestial bodies, but as debris. Some astrophysicists describe comets as 'dirty snowballs', with tails of gas and dust. Folly's Comet has an icy nucleus of cold-war delirium and an immense tail of political gas.

ABBREVIATIONS AND ACRONYMS

ABM	anti-ballistic missile
ACDA	Arms Control and Disarmament Agency
ASAT	anti-satellite weapon
ATM	anti-tactical missile (sometimes ATBM)
BMD	ballistic missile defence
C^3I	command, control, communications and intelligence
DSAT	satellite defence
EMP	electromagnetic pulse
ICBM	intercontinental ballistic missile
LOW	launch on warning
MAD	mutual assured destruction
MIRV	multiple independently targeted re-entry vehicle
NORAD	North American Air Defense Command
NPT	Non-Proliferation Treaty
NTM	national technical means (of verification)
NUDETS	nuclear detection system
NUTS	nuclear utilization target selection
PAR	phased-array radar
PTBT	Partial Test Ban Treaty
SAC	Strategic Air Command
SALT	Strategic Arms Limitations Talks (& agreements)
SAM	surface-to-air missiles
SCC	Standing Consultative Commission (for SALT)
SDI	Strategic Defence Initiative
SDIO	SDI Organization
SLBM	submarine-launched ballistic missiles
TDI	Tactical Defence Initiative
USAF	United States Air Force
WWMCCS	World-Wide Military Command and Control System

Notes

Chapter 1

1. Weinberger, 'Meet the Press', 27 March 1983; *Bulletin of the Atomic Scientists*, June–July 1983.
2. Union of Concerned Scientists (ed. John Tirman), *The Fallacy of Star Wars*, New York, 1984, p. 51; McGeorge Bundy, George Kennan, Robert McNamara and Gerard Smith in *Foreign Affairs*, Winter 1984, p. 264.
3. Philip M. Boffey, 'Star Wars and Mankind', *NY Times*, 8 March 1985; *The President's Strategic Defense Initiative*, Washington DC, White House, January 1985, p. 4.
4. George W. Ball, 'The War for Star Wars', *NY Review of Books*, 11 April 1985.
5. Leslie H. Gelb, 'Vision of Space Defense', *NY Times*, 3 March 1985.
6. William J. Broad, 'Reagan's Star Wars Bid', *NY Times*, 4 March 1985.
7. Broad, op. cit.; Ball, op. cit.; Paul B. Stares, *Space Weapons and US Strategy: Origins and Development*, London, 1985, p. 225.
8. J. Killian, *Sputnik, Scientists and Eisenhower*, Cambridge, Mass., 1977, p. 57.
9. Khrushchev and Biriuzov are cited in Stares, op. cit., pp. 74–5, 80, on whose detailed account of satellite and ASAT developments these paragraphs draw heavily.
10. Stares, op. cit., p. 35.
11. ibid., p. 65; Walter A. McDougall, 'Sputnik, the Space Race, and the Cold War', *Bulletin of the Atomic Scientists*, May 1985. See Herbert F. York, 'Nuclear Deterrence and the Military Use of Space', *Dædalus*, Spring 1985: 'our space programmes, *from the beginning*, have been primarily of a military, not a civilian or scientific nature'.
12. J. B. Wiesner and H. F. York, cited in Rip Bulkeley, *The Anti-Ballistic Missile Treaty, 1972–83*, University of Bradford School of Peace Studies, 1984.
13. Vincent Mosco, 'Star Wars/Earth Wars', *Issues in Radical Science*, 17, 1985, pp. 36–7; Philip M. Boffey, 'Pressures are Increasing for Arms Race in Space', *NY Times*, 18 October 1982; William Scobie, 'Reagan's Star Wars Dream', *Observer*, 27 June 1982; Stares, op. cit., pp. 206–24.
14. Robert Scheer, *With Enough Shovels*, New York, 1982, pp. 104, 250–51.
15. See Richard Burt, 'Arms and the Man', in *Reagan the Man, the President* (*NY Times*, Election Special), 1980, pp. 86–9.
16. Norman Moss, 'Sunday with Edward Teller', *Listener*, 13 June 1985.
17. Edward Teller to the President, cited in William J. Broad, *NY Times*, 4 March 1985. An account of the X-ray laser test appeared in *Aviation Week & Space Technology*, 23 February 1981.

18. Broad, op. cit.

19. Committee of Soviet Scientists for Peace against Nuclear Threat, 'Strategic and International-Political Consequences of Creating a Space-Based Anti-Missile System using Directed Energy Weapons', typescript, Moscow, 1984, p. 12.

20. Philip M. Boffey in *NY Times*, 18 October 1982; *NY Times*, 30 March 1983. See also the fascinating account of the Livermore Laboratory in William Broad, 'The Scientists of Star Wars', *Granta*, 16, 1985.

21. *Aviation Week*, 8 March 1982.

22. See Christopher Paine, 'Running in Circles with MX', *Bulletin of the Atomic Scientists*, December 1981, and the same author's 'MX: Too Dense for Congress', ibid., February 1983. Also Scheer, op. cit., Chapter 6, 'Window of Vulnerability'.

23. Weinberger, *Annual Report to Congress, Fiscal Year 1985*, p. 193.

24. See Bulkeley, op. cit., pp. 16–18; *The Fallacy of Star Wars*, op. cit., pp. 10–16; Christopher Paine in *Bulletin of the Atomic Scientists*, February 1983; R. J. Smith, 'Carter's Plan for MX Lives On', *Science*, 30 April 1982.

25. See David Watt, 'Wishful Thinking on a Star', *The Times*, 15 February 1985.

26. Leslie H. Gelb in *NY Times*, 3 March 1985.

27. *Aviation Week & Space Technology*, 8 March 1982.

28. ibid., 25 May 1981; Broad, op. cit.

29. Dr Keyworth, the President's science adviser, and Robert C. McFarlane, now National Security Adviser (and then Deputy Adviser), have also been credited with writing parts of the crucial sections of the speech. Gerold Yonas, Chief Scientist of the SDIO, confirms the influence on SDI planning of the MX-basing problem and of the pressure of the Freeze Movement and the Catholic bishops in *Dædalus*, Spring 1985, p. 74.

30. *Boston Globe*, 13 May 1984; William Scobie in *Observer*, 27 June 1982.

Chapter 2

1. *Arms Control in Space: Workshop Proceedings*, Washington DC, US Office of Technology Assessment, May 1984.

2. ABM Treaty, 1972, Article VI(a).

3. *New Scientist*, 21 January 1985.

4. Robert M. Bowman, 'How BMD? Why BMD?', Institute for Space and Security Studies, September 1984.

5. Union of Concerned Scientists (ed. John Tirman), *The Fallacy of Star Wars*, New York, 1984, p. 101.

6. Kosta Tsipsis, *Understanding Nuclear Weapons*, London, 1985, p. 103.

7. *The Fallacy of Star Wars*, op. cit., p. 103.

8. ibid., p. 137.

9. Ashton B. Carter, *Directed Energy Missile Defense in Space*, Washington DC, US Office of Technology Assessment, April 1984. These estimates, as well as certain estimates of the Union of Concerned Scientists, have encountered fierce criticisms from the SDI lobby (especially from within the Livermore Laboratory) and supporters. The estimates vary widely with the data-base and consequent parameters, and emphasize the hypothetical nature of the whole exercise: see Robert Jastrow, 'The War against "Star Wars" ', *Commentary*, December 1984, and seventeen pages on both sides of the question in *Commentary*, March 1985; and Frank von Hippel in *Bulletin of the Atomic Scientists*, April 1985.

10. *Guardian*, 26 July 1985.

11. An active 'Space Policeman' probe has been suggested, which would irradiate a satellite with neutrons, and attempt to detect whether or not a nuclear warhead was present by the number of neutrons emitted by the target.

12. R. Jeffrey Smith, 'The Search for Nuclear Sanctuary', *Science*, 1 and 8 July 1983.

13. 'Space Litter Making Life Hazardous for Orbiting Visitors', *International Herald Tribune*, 30 March 1985.

14. *The Fallacy of Star Wars*, op. cit., p. 225.

15. *Space Based Missile Defense*, Union of Concerned Scientists, March 1984.

16. *The Strategic Defense Initiative: Costs, Contractors and Consequences*, New York, Council on Economic Priorities, 1985.

17. Desmond Ball, 'Can Nuclear War Be Controlled?' (Adelphi Paper 169), London, International Institute of Strategic Studies, 1981. See also Ashton B. Carter, 'The Command and Control of Nuclear War', *Scientific American*, January 1985.

18. Bowman, op. cit.

19. Daniel Ford, 'The Button', *New Yorker*, 1 May 1985.

20. Peter Pringle and William Arkin, *SIOP: Nuclear War from the Inside*, London, 1983, p. 97.

21. ibid., p. 111.

22. Ball, op. cit., p. 13.

23. *Sunday Times*, 30 June 1985. In July Professor David Parnas resigned from the SDIO advisory panel on 'computing in support of battle management', saying the commission was impossible and it would never be possible to test the array of computers under realistic conditions: 'it is our duty as scientists and engineers' to tell the President and the public that 'we have no technological magic': *NY Times*, 12 July 1985.

24. Daniel Deudney, *Space: the High Frontier in Perspective* (Worldwatch Paper 50), Washington DC, August 1982, quoting a panel of experts at the American Institute of Aeronautics and Astronautics.

25. 'The Trouble with "Star Wars" ', Institute for Space and Security Studies, September 1983.

Chapter 3

Although the Soviet BMD programme has been the subject of considerable public debate, substantive descriptions of this programme are remarkably few in number. The standard beginning point is the *Soviet Military Power* booklet produced each year by the US Defense Intelligence Agency, although the factual detail about current activities is occasionally difficult to separate from the alarmist speculation on future developments.

Probably the most comprehensive description of the Soviet programme is contained in the book *The Impact of U.S. and Soviet Ballistic Missile Defense Programs on the ABM Treaty*, published by the National Campaign to Save the ABM Treaty (Washington, DC). Another useful treatment is the chapter 'The Soviet BMD Program' by Sayre Stevens in *Ballistic Missile Defense* by Ashton Carter and David Schwartz (Brookings, 1984).

The best discussion of Soviet air defence is by David R. Jones in the various editions of the *Soviet Armed Forces Review Annual.* John Collins of the Congressional Research Service provides the best enumeration of Soviet air defence forces in his recent *US-Soviet Military Balance 1980–1985.*

A good overview of the early controversy over the Soviet directed-energy-weapon programme is contained in 'Charged Debate Erupts over Russian Beam Weapon' by Nicholas Wade in *Science*, 27 May 1977, pages 957–9. A recent description of the Soviet programme is in Roger Main's 'The USSR and Laser Weaponry: the View from Outside' in *Defense Systems Review*, vol. 3, no. 3, 1985. Paul Stares provides an excellent history of the Soviet anti-satellite weapon programme in *The Militarization of Space – US Policy, 1945–84* (Croom-Helm, 1985).

Chapter 4

1. Foreword to 'The President's Strategic Defence Initiative', White House, January 1985.
2. Harold Brown, 'The Strategic Defence Initiative', *Survival,* March/April 1985, p. 62.
3. Paul Nitze, 'The Objectives of Arms Control', *Survival,* May/June 1985, pp. 105–6.
4. J. Goldblat, *Agreements for Arms Control*, London, 1982, p. 355.
5. Gen. Bernard Schriever, Address to the USAF Academy Symposium on Military Space Doctrine, 1–3 April 1981, in *The Great Frontier*, ed. Maj. P. Viotti *et al.*, p. 34.

6. Commonwealth Prime Ministers' Statement on Disarmament, March 1961, 3-c. Similar wording was adopted for the Joint Statement of Principles for Disarmament by the Soviet Union and the United States (the 'McCloy–Zorin Agreement') six months later.

7. H. Smith *et al.*, *Reagan the Man, the President*, New York, MacMillan, 1980, p. 87.

8. *International Herald Tribune*, 28 May 1981.

9. *Report to Congress on Prospects for Anti-Satellite Limitations*, April 1984.

10. Interview on ABC television, 8 April 1984.

11. R. J. Smith, 'Carter's Plan for MX Lives On', *Science*, 30 April 1982.

12. *FAS Public Interest Report*, March 1985, p. 3.

13. *Bulletin of Atomic Science*, 8 October 1982.

14. *NY Times*, 31 May 1984.

15. Article by Robert Scheer, *LA Times*, 4 October 1981.

16. Interview with Ken Auletta, *NY Daily News*, 24 May 1981.

17. Interview with J. W. Canan, *US Air Force Magazine*, June 1984.

18. *Pittsburgh Press*, 13 June 1984.

19. Article in *Strategic Review*, 1979.

20. Article in *Richmond Times Despatch*, 7 March 1984.

21. *Aviation Week & Space Technology*, 8 March 1982.

22. Quoted by J. W. Canan in *Air Force Magazine*, June 1984.

23. W. J. Broad, 'The Young Physicists', *NY Times*, 31 January 1984.

24. Report of interview with S. A. Tremaine, Deputy for Development Planning, Aeronautical Systems Division, Air Force Systems Command, in Canan, ibid.

25. Address to the American Association for the Advancement of Science, 29 May 1984.

26. S. Drell, P. Farley and D. Holloway, 'The Reagan Strategic Defence Initiative: a Technical, Political and Arms Control Assessment', Special Report of the Stanford University Center for International Security and Arms Control, July 1984, p. 62.

27. P. M. Boffey, 'Dark Side of "Star Wars": System Could Also Attack', *NY Times*, 7 March 1985.

28. B. Jasani, 'The Arms Control Dilemma – an Overview', p. 40, in B. Jasani, ed., *Space Weapons – the Arms Control Dilemma*, SIPRI, 1984.

29. For those wanting more detail, we recommend the still succinct narrative in Paul Stares, *Space Weapons and US Strategy*, London, 1985, pp. 229–35, on which our own account is partly based.

30. Rostow's words are cited from the Senate Sub-Committee hearing on 20 September 1982 in Stares, op. cit., p. 230.

31. Texts of the two Soviet draft treaties are in Jasani, op. cit., pp. 243–7. For analyses, see contributions to that volume; also, the Annex by R. V. Strode,

pp. 85–91, in C. Gray, *American Space Policy*, 1982; J. Pike, 'Limits on Space Weapons: the Soviet Initiative and the American Response', FAS Staff Study, 12 September 1983; and Stares, op. cit.

32. Patricia M. Mische, *Star Wars and the State of Our Souls*, Minneapolis, 1985, p. 66; see also her study, *Do the Soviets Cheat at Arms Control?*.

33. Reports in *NY Post* and *NY Times*, 13 June 1984.

34. *Washington Post*, 16 June 1984.

35. Stares, op. cit., p. 235.

36. *NY News*, 25 March 1983.

37. *Pravda* interview, 27 March 1983, in Drell *et al.*, op. cit., p. 105.

38. Mische, *Star Wars and the State of Our Souls*, op. cit., p. 73.

39. T. K. Longstreth, J. E. Pike and J. B. Rhinelander, *Impact of U.S. and Soviet Ballistic Missile Defence Programmes on the ABM Treaty*, 1985, p. 26. This is by far the most thorough treatment of these issues now available, and indispensable for anyone wishing to probe them further.

40. P. Tyler, 'War In Space', *Washington Post*, 3 April 1984, D 1 & 4.

41. ACDA, *Arms Control Impact Statement FY1979*, p. 231 n. 3.

42. Testimony to House Armed Services Committee, 24 February 1982.

43. *NY Times*, 25 March 1983.

44. Mische, *Star Wars and the State of Our Souls*, op. cit., pp. 70–72 for summary and references.

45. Quotations are from official excerpts from the February 1985 report, *Soviet Noncompliance with Arms Control Agreements*, USIS, 5 February 1985.

46. *Daily Telegraph*, 16 March 1985; *Observer*, 24 April 1985; Lawrence Freedman, *The Times*, 24 July 1985.

47. Longstreth *et al.*, op. cit., p. 41.

48. Remarks to the Congressional Advisory Board of the American Security Council, 4 June 1985.

49. Address to the AGM of the European Atlantic Group, 17 June 1985, 'The Impact of the Strategic Defence Initiative on the Western Alliance'.

50. Both from Senate Armed Services Committee hearings, February 1984, in *Science*, 10 August 1984, pp. 600–601.

51. Senior Soviet Air Force strategist Gen. V. A. Shatalov, interview with *United News of India*, 14 May 1984.

52. From R. Sagdayev *et al.*, Committee of Soviet Scientists for Peace against Nuclear Threat, 'A Space-Based Anti-Missile System with Directed-Energy Weapons: Strategic, Legal and Political Implications' (excerpts), *Survival*, March/April 1985.

53. 'NPT Prohibitions on the Transfer and Development of Nuclear Explosive-Based Defensive Weapons', memorandum by Eldon Greenberg, 25 June 1985.

54. Sir Geoffrey Howe, 'Defence and Security in the Nuclear Age', speech given at the Royal United Services Institute, 15 March 1985.

55. 'New Technology and Western Security Policy', paper to 26th Annual Conference of the IISS, September 1984.

Chapter 5

1. Patricia M. Mische, *Star Wars and the State of Our Souls*, Minneapolis, 1985, p. 7.

2. Matthew Rothschild and Keenen Peck, 'Star Wars', *The Progressive*, July 1985, p. 26.

3. Robert D. Bowman, 'Star Wars and Arms Control', Institute for Space and Strategic Studies, 1985.

4. The undated document on Heritage Foundation paper is marked 'In-house, Secret' and 'Not for Release'. A copy found its way to the American and European peace movements, and extracts were published also in *Harper's*, June 1985. W. B. Weinrod of the Heritage Foundation claims it was a High Frontier document, and disclaims Heritage responsibility: *Guardian*, letters, 27 July 1985.

5. Mische, op. cit., p. 75.

6. *Washington Times*, 17 May 1984.

7. *Hartford Courant*, 5 April 1985.

8. Wayne Biddle in *NY Sunday Times*, 30 December 1984; US Department of Defense, *Near-Term Demonstrations and Deployments*, April 1984.

9. 'The Myths of Edward Teller', *Bulletin of the Atomic Scientists*, March 1983.

10. William A. Davis, jr, 'Current Technical Status of US BMD Programs' in M. Marcoviller, ed., *U.S. Arms Control Objectives and the Implication for Ballistic Missile Defense*, Harvard University, 1980.

11. *The Progressive*, July 1985, p. 22.

12. See Charles Mohr in *NY Times*, 7 May 1985; Sidney Drell and Gerard C Smith, *NY Times*, 13 May 1985; *Guardian*, 25 May 1985.

13. *NY Times*, 14 July 1985.

14. Charles Mohr in *NY Times*, 6 July 1985.

15. See Malcolm Dando and Paul Rogers, *The Death of Deterrence*, CND 1984; Howard Morland, 'Are We Readying for a First Strike?', *The Nation*, 16 March 1985.

16. *The Progressive*, July 1985, p. 22.

17. Edward Teller in F. J. Ossenbeck and Patricia C. Kraeck, eds., *Open Space and Peace*, Stanford, Hoover Institute, 1964, p. 199.

18. The Pentagon has acknowledged the risk of a nuclear winter in a preliminary study, 'The Potential Effects of Nuclear War on the Climate': see

Wayne Biddle in *NY Times*, 2 March 1985. Two armchair geniuses have even used the nuclear winter as an argument for SDI: it would reduce the number of nuclear explosions within the atmosphere to a 'safe' level: Paine and Gray, 'Nuclear Policy and the Defensive Transition', *Foreign Affairs*, vol. 62, pp. 819–42.

19. It is one sign of the profound ideological corruption of much American and West European academic strategic theory that its projections are always founded upon the need to 'deter' a hypothetical Soviet disarming first strike, whereas the counter-hypothesis of a United States first disarming strike is usually dismissed as sensational Communist propaganda.

20. Reagan interview in *Newsweek*, 18 March 1985.

21. Edward Teller, 'The Role of Space and Defence in the NATO Alliance', in *NATO's Sixteen Nations*, November 1984.

22. *Foreign Affairs*, Summer 1985.

23. W. J. Broad in *NY Times*, 13 May 1985.

24. See W. J. Broad, 'Allies in Europe are Apprehensive about Benefits of Star Wars', *NY Times*, 13 May 1985. Measured statements of European objections to SDI by adherents of deterrence theory and arms control will be found in International Institute of Strategic Studies, *Strategic Survey, 1984–5*; Peter David, *'Star Wars' and Arms Control*, Council for Arms Control, July 1985; Lawrence Freedman, 'NATO and the Strategic Defense Initiative', *NATO's Sixteen Nations*, November 1984.

25. Unfortunately we cannot reveal all our sources for these high goings-on, but see *Guardian*, 22 December 1984.

26. *Guardian*, 21 February 1985; *NY Times*, 16 March 1985.

27. Robert G. Herman and Carol V. Rose in *Arms Control Today*, July/August 1984.

28. See *Guardian* leader, 24 July 1985; also Zbigniew Brzezinski, Robert Jastrow, Max Kampelman, 'Search for Security: The Case for the Strategic Defense Initiative', *International Herald Tribune*, 28 January 1985.

29. *Guardian*, 11 February 1985. The French government had opposed SDI (as putting 'dissuasion' in jeopardy) at the Geneva disarmament conference in June 1984. Mitterrand developed proposals for a European counter to SDI as early as February 1984: see *Le Monde*, 9 February, 18 December 1984.

30. The Norwegian parliament has opposed plans for SDI deployment and urged resumed negotiations to prohibit weapons in space, but rejected (by 75 to 74 votes) a motion to oppose research (4 June 1985: 'Nuclear Disarmament News', Nei til atomvapen, Oslo, June 1985). On 14 May 1985 the anti-government majority in the Danish parliament passed a motion not to take part in SDI: *De Waarheid*, 15 May 1985. For Australia, see T. B. Millar in *Dædalus*, Summer 1985.

31. The Free Democratic Party took a strongly critical position on SDI, thus strengthening Herr Genscher against Chancellor Kohl: *Guardian*, 3 June 1985.

32. Leslie Gelb in *NY Times*, 3 March 1985.

33. *NY Times*, 16 March 1985.

34. See Strobe Talbot, *Deadly Gambits*, New York, 1984.

35. The Hon. Richard Perle, address of 19 March 1985 (mimeograph).

36. The 'Beyond 1984' conference was observed by Walter Schwarz in *Guardian*, 22 March 1985.

37. W. J. Broad in *NY Times*, 13 May 1985.

38. *The Times*, 28 March 1985. A conference was organized in Rotterdam jointly by 'High Frontier Europe' and the European Security Institute (EIS) with General Gallois and Air Vice-Marshal Menaul among the speakers: *Trouw*, 22 June 1985.

39. George W. Ball, 'The War for Star Wars', *NY Review of Books*, 11 April 1985.

40. *The Times*, leader, 25 June 1985.

41. See Edward Schumacher in *NY Times*, 7 June 1985, and *Guardian* and *The Times* of same date; Leslie Gelb, *NY Times*, 9 June 1985.

42. *Guardian*, 20 June 1985, reporting a new State Department sales brochure.

43. *The Times*, 25 June 1985.

44. See *Guardian*, 27 May and 21 and 26 June 1985; Leslie Gelb in *NY Times*, 3 July 1985.

45. Estimate of a spokesman for Philips in *NRC-Handelsblad*, 25 June 1985.

46. Lawrence Freedman has pointed out that British industry has won only $30 million worth of contracts out of the $4 billion programme for Britain's very own Trident D-5: *New Statesman*, 5 July 1985, p. 18.

47. *Der Spiegel*, 20 August 1984.

48. *Der Spiegel*, 10 December 1984.

49. *The Times*, leader, 19 March 1985.

50. Interview in *Libération*, 3 May 1985.

51. *Guardian*, 29 May 1985; *NY Times*, 21 May 1985; *The Times*, 21 May 1985.

52. Profile of General James Abrahamson, *The Times*, 16 May 1985; 'A Marketing Blitz in Western Europe', *Newsweek*, 17 June 1985.

53. See e.g. *Newsweek*, ibid., and Peter van Deutekom and Theo Koele in *Trouw*, 29 June 1985.

54. *NRC-Handelsblad*, 25 June 1985.

55. *Die Zeit*, 19 April 1985.

56. *Libération*, 25 June 1985.

57. Wubbo Tempel in *NRC-Handelsblad*, 1 May 1985.

58. As set forward in the French prospectus, 'Eureka: The Technological Renaissance of Europe', June 1985.

59. E. G. Lachman in *NCR-Handelsblad*, 27 June 1985.
60. Anthony Tucker, 'Who Really Needs Eureka?', *Guardian*, 1 August 1985.
61. *NCR-Handelsblad*, 25 May 1985.
62. Interview between General Abrahamson and General Gallios, *Géopolitique*, 9, Spring 1985. There are also times when military high-tech, like nuclear waste, is able to transcend the bloc division: General Abrahamson told reporters that the main particle-beam device at Los Alamos works 'because there are three separate Soviet inventions included in that weapon': William J. Broad in *NY Times*, 1 July 1985.
63. *Libération*, 4 and 5 June 1985. British Plessey are also tendering with Rockwell as contractors for the Ptarmigan system.
64. *Die Zeit*, 19 April 1985.
65. See *Le Monde*, 9–10 June 1985.
66. *Guardian*, 23 July 1985.
67. *Le Monde*, 9–10 June 1985. For the alarming developments already on the way, see Paul Hoag, 'High Technology Army Weaponry', *Economic Forum*, Summer 1982.
68. *Géopolitique*, loc. cit.
69. *NY Times*, 13 May 1985.
70. *Géopolitique*, op. cit.; David M. Abshire, 'SDI – The Path to a More Mature Deterrent', *NATO Review*, April 1985; *Trouw*, 22 June 1985.
71. *Trouw*, 29 June 1985.
72. Rip Bulkeley in a paper, 'Forward Basing – The Secret Key to SDI?', July 1985, unpublished.
73. *Voice of America*, 8 July 1985.
74. Lawrence Freedman in *The Times*, 24 July 1985; T. K. Longstreth, J. E. Pike, and J. B. Rhinelander, *Impact of U.S. and Soviet Ballistic Missile Defence Programmes on the ABM Treaty*, 1985, pp. 40–41.
75. *NY Times*, 19 March 1985. The words 'some might be here' (i.e. in Canada) were omitted from the transcript provided by the US Embassy in Ottawa: *NY Times*, 20 March 1985.
76. Interview in *La Vie Française*, 1–7 July 1985.
77. *NY Times*, 29 May and 1 June 1985; *De Volkskrant*, 30 May 1985.
78. For example, Marshal Sokolov in *Guardian*, 6 May 1985.
79. W. J. Broad in *NY Times*, 13 May 1985. See Christoph Bertram, 'Strategic Defense and the Western Alliance', *Dædalus*, Summer 1985, p. 285.
80. *Sunday Times*, 26 May 1985. When Trident is deployed, British warheads could increase from the current 64 to as many as 896 in the 1990s: Bertram, op. cit., p. 285.
81. See e.g. *Guardian*, 26 July 1985.
82. *Progressive*, July 1985, p. 23.
83. *NY Times*, 2 June 1985.

84. *Times*, 11 June 1985.
85. See Leslie Gelb in *NY Times*, 8 July; *Guardian*, 9 and 10 July; *Times*, 26 July; Seth Mydans in *NY Times*, 26 July 1985.
86. Leslie Gelb in *NY Times*, 4 July 1985.
87. *Le Monde*, 23 May 1985.
88. Gelb in *NY Times*, 4 July 1985.
89. William E. Borrows, 'Ballistic Missile Defense: the Illusion of Security', *Foreign Affairs*, Spring 1984.
90. Solly Zuckerman, 'Nuclear War: Can Anything Stop the Rain?', *NY Times Book Review*, 20 January 1985.
91. William J. Broad in *NY Times*, 1 July 1985, citing the Fletcher Committee's Report, and commenting on research at CERN.
92. Reported by the Tel Aviv correspondent of the Dutch 'quality' paper, *NRC-Handelsblad*, 2 May 1985. This could be related to the restoration of US programmes for very heavy carrier rockets – Titan cargo missiles: Sjoerd van der Werf, *NRC-Handelsblad*, 4 May 1985.
93. See 'The Star Warriors' in *Newsweek*, 17 June 1985.
94. ibid.
95. Institute for Space and Security Studies newsletter, June 1985.
96. Philip M. Boffey, 'The Dark Side of Star Wars', *NY Times*, 7 March 1985. A source with years of experience in military space projects said that space-to-ground weapons are 'probably one of the most sensitive aspects' of the space-shuttle programme: see *Progressive*, July 1985, p. 22; also Mische, op. cit., pp. 10, 43.
97. *Wall Street Journal*, 2 January 1985.
98. John Pike's estimates in 'The Strategic Defense Initiative: Budget and Program', Washington DC, February 1985, were revised upwards in June 1985; see also *NY Times*, 13 June 1985.
99. William D. Hartung and others, *The Strategic Defense Initiative: Costs, Contractors and Consequences*, a valuable study by the Council on Economic Priorities, New York, 1985, p. 150.
100. *NY Times*, 17 January 1985.
101. Hartung and others, op. cit.
102. These firms were already involved in BMD developments: Lockheed with the Homing Overlay Experiment, McDonnell Douglas with the Low-Altitude Defense System, and LTV in Small Radar Homing Technology (SR-HIT): see pp. 152, 188–92.
103. ibid., p. 29.
104. ibid., pp. 175, 186.
105. David E. Sanger, *NY Times*, 22 July 1985; *NY Times*, 18 May 1985.
106. See Sanger, op. cit.; Harold Jackson in *Guardian*, 7 June 1985.
107. Robert Chesshyre in *Observer*, 26 May 1985.

108. These paragraphs draw on Thomas Karas, *The New High Ground: Systems and Weapons of Space Age War*, New York, 1983, pp. 48–58.

109. See Eric R. Alterman in *NY Times*, 11 July 1985: 'the Pentagon has funded close to 40 per cent of all the research and development in the United States. The comparable figure in Japan is less than 1 per cent; yet Japan exports $5 billion more in high-tech products to the United States than it imports from us. Japan's share of the world's high-tech markets tripled between 1962 and 1979, while our share declined by nearly one-third.'

110. Mary Kaldor, *The Baroque Arsenal*, London, 1981.

111. *Newsweek*, 17 June 1985, p. 19. See also Mische, op. cit., p. 10.

112. Jack Mendelsohn in *New Statesman*, 5 July 1985.

113. On these exposures of Pentagon inefficiency, and of arms contractors' bribery, fraud and scandalous profit levels – which seriously dented Weinberger's image in 1985 – see *Observer*, 26 May 1985; Nicholas Ashford in *The Times*, 23 May 1985.

114. *The Progressive*, July 1985, p. 26.

115. See Union of Concerned Scientists, *The Fallacy of Star Wars*, New York, 1984, p. 28.

116. David Watt in *The Times*, 15 February 1985.

117. See Dan Smith in *New Statesman*, 12 July 1985, and the Harris Poll reported in *Hartford Courant*, 5 April 1985 (men favoured Star Wars 'by 3 points' but women opposed it 'by 34 points').

118. Council for Economic Priorities, newsletter, October 1984.

119. 'The Case for Star Wars', *Economist*, 3 August 1985.

120. Caesar Voute, of the Institute for Advanced Strategic Research, Lowestoft, in a private communication to the author.

121. *NY Times*, 5, 6 September 1985.

122. 'An Interview with Gorbachev', *Time*, 9 September 1985.

123. See William J. Broad in *NY Times*, 1 July 1985.

124. In addition to draft treaties tabled by the Soviet Union and other nations in the United Nations, an ASAT Treaty has been proposed by the Union of Concerned Scientists, and the Federation of American Scientists is among bodies suggesting amendments to both, or revisions of the ABM Treaty. Greenpeace International has issued proposals to strengthen the Non-Proliferation Treaty.

125. *The Times*, 9 September 1985.

126. *Guardian*, 12 September 1985.

127. *Sunday Times*, 8 September 1985; *Guardian*, 9 September 1985.

128. *The Times*, 9 September 1985.

129. *Sunday Times*, 8 September 1985.

130. Gerold Yonas, 'The Strategic Defense Initiative', *Dædalus*, Spring 1985, p. 89.

131. *Guardian*, 28 September 1985.
132. Eloquent proposals for returning to peaceful international cooperation in space are in Daniel Deudney, *Space: The High Frontier in Perspective* (Worldwatch Paper 50), Washington DC, 1982; Spark M. Matsunaga, 'U.S.–Soviet Space Co-operation', *Bulletin of the Atomic Scientists*, March 1985; Mische, op. cit.; and Deudney, 'Forging Weapons into Spaceships', *World Policy Journal*, Spring 1985.
133. Gerard Manley Hopkins, 'God's Grandeur'.

Acknowledgements

This book started its life as a booklet, by Ben and Edward Thompson, *Star Wars: Self-Destruct Incorporated*, published in May 1985 by Merlin Press. The first two sections of this have been revised and extended for Chapters 1 and 2 of the present book. The third section has been rewritten, to take in new material on European responses to Star Wars, Eureka, and the American space-arms contractors (Chapter 5). But the book still had two serious gaps. John Pike, the Associate Director for Space Policy at the Federation of American Scientists, responded to our urgent requests and sent us an expert assessment of space-related military developments by the Soviet Union (Chapter 3). And Rip Bulkeley laid other work aside to supply an equally expert account of the effect of SDI on arms-control agreements and disarmament.

The three British contributors worked as partners and exchanged material with one another. But each is responsible for the conclusions in his own chapter. We are honoured to have Professor Dorothy Hodgkin in our pages, but she is certainly not responsible for our opinions (or any possible errors). John Pike, in the conditions of American political debate, is an eloquent and prominent defender of the arms-control process, and does not share the scepticism towards arms control expressed at other places in this book. Editorial planning was shared by Ben and Edward Thompson as co-editors, but in the book's final stages Edward Thompson edited the copy for the press, and is responsible for its final form.

We have received the most generous help from many friends, and it is not possible to acknowledge everyone. We must thank Martin Eve and Sarah Tisdall, of Merlin Press, and Louis Mackay, for giving the book launch-off. Among others who answered inquiries, exchanged material and criticized drafts, are Christopher Meredith and Graham Spinardi of SANA (Scientists Against Nuclear Arms); Stephen Brown of CND International Committee and the CND Information Service; Colin Hines and Greenpeace International; Andrew Franklin of

Penguin Books; Denis Hall, James Hinton, Jane Mayes, Conor Minague, Paul Rogers, Dorothy Thompson, Andrew White and John Williams.

International briefings have been of the first importance. We have received generous help from the specialist groups of END (European Nuclear Disarmament) and from END's network of international friends. Particular thanks go to W. H. Ferry, END's representative in the United States, who has sent us weekly briefings and materials throughout 1985; to friends in the Federation of American Scientists and the Union of Concerned Scientists; to Patricia and Paul Chilton and Jolyon Howorth of END's French working group, and to Philippe Laublet and to CODENE; to Ausma Acworth for monitoring and translating German material and to Patrick Burke of END's German working group; and to Caesar Voute, who sent us valuable suggestions as well as extensive translations from the Dutch press. In appreciation for this help, and in acknowledgement of the collective nature of this project, the contributors have all agreed to pass on the greater part of the royalties from the book to END, whose address is now 11 Goodwin Street, London N4 3HQ.

EPT

MORE ABOUT PENGUINS, PELICANS, PEREGRINES AND PUFFINS

For further information about books available from Penguins please write to Dept EP, Penguin Books Ltd, Harmondsworth, Middlesex UB7 0DA.

In the U.S.A.: For a complete list of books available from Penguins in the United States write to Dept DG, Penguin Books, 299 Murray Hill Parkway, East Rutherford, New Jersey 07073.

In Canada: For a complete list of books available from Penguins in Canada write to Penguin Books Canada Ltd, 2801 John Street, Markham, Ontario L3R 1B4.

In Australia: For a complete list of books available from Penguins in Australia write to the Marketing Department, Penguin Books Australia Ltd, P.O. Box 257, Ringwood, Victoria 3134.

In New Zealand: For a complete list of books available from Penguins in New Zealand write to the Marketing Department, Penguin Books (N.Z.) Ltd, Private Bag, Takapuna, Auckland 9.

In India: For a complete list of books available from Penguins in India write to Penguin Overseas Ltd, 706 Eros Apartments, 56 Nehru Place, New Delhi 110019.

THE PENGUIN ENGLISH DICTIONARY

The Penguin English Dictionary has been created specially for today's needs. It features:

* More entries than any other popularly priced dictionary
* Exceptionally clear and precise definitions
* For the first time in an equivalent dictionary, the internationally recognised IPA pronunciation system
* Emphasis on contemporary usage
* Extended coverage of both the spoken and the written word
* Scientific tables
* Technical words
* Informal and colloquial expressions
* Vocabulary most widely used *wherever* English is spoken
* Most commonly used abbreviations

It is twenty years since the publication of the last English dictionary by Penguin and the compilation of this entirely new *Penguin English Dictionary* is the result of a special collaboration between Longman, one of the world's leading dictionary publishers, and Penguin Books. The material is based entirely on the database of the acclaimed *Longman Dictionary of the English Language.*

1008 pages   051.139 3   £2.50 ☐

PENGUIN REFERENCE BOOKS

☐ **The Penguin Map of the World** £2.50

Clear, colourful, crammed with information and fully up-to-date, this is a useful map to stick on your wall at home, at school or in the office.

☐ **The Penguin Map of Europe** £2.95

Covers all land eastwards to the Urals, southwards to North Africa and up to Syria, Iraq and Iran * Scale = 1:5,500,000 * 4-colour artwork * Features main roads, railways, oil and gas pipelines, plus extra information including national flags, currencies and populations.

☐ **The Penguin Map of the British Isles** £1.95

Including the Orkneys, the Shetlands, the Channel Islands and much of Normandy, this excellent map is ideal for planning routes and touring holidays, or as a study aid.

☐ **The Penguin Dictionary of Quotations** £3.95

A treasure-trove of over 12,000 new gems and old favourites, from Aesop and Matthew Arnold to Xenophon and Zola.

☐ **The Penguin Dictionary of Art and Artists** £3.95

Fifth Edition. 'A vast amount of information intelligently presented, carefully detailed, abreast of current thought and scholarship and easy to read' – *The Times Literary Supplement*

☐ **The Penguin Pocket Thesaurus** £1.95

A pocket-sized version of Roget's classic, and an essential companion for all commuters, crossword addicts, students, journalists and the stuck-for-words.

A CHOICE OF PENGUINS

☐ **The Complete Penguin Stereo Record and Cassette Guide**
Greenfield, Layton and March £7.95

A new edition, now including information on compact discs. 'One of the few indispensables on the record collector's bookshelf' – *Gramophone*

☐ **Selected Letters of Malcolm Lowry**
Edited by Harvey Breit and Margerie Bonner Lowry £5.95

'Lowry emerges from these letters not only as an extremely interesting man, but also a lovable one' – Philip Toynbee

☐ **The First Day on the Somme**
Martin Middlebrook £3.95

1 July 1916 was the blackest day of slaughter in the history of the British Army. 'The soldiers receive the best service a historian can provide: their story told in their own words' – *Guardian*

☐ **A Better Class of Person** **John Osborne** £1.95

The playwright's autobiography, 1929–56. 'Splendidly enjoyable' – John Mortimer. 'One of the best, richest and most bitterly truthful autobiographies that I have ever read' – Melvyn Bragg

☐ **The Winning Streak** **Goldsmith and Clutterbuck** £2.95

Marks & Spencer, Saatchi & Saatchi, United Biscuits, GEC ... The UK's top companies reveal their formulas for success, in an important and stimulating book that no British manager can afford to ignore.

☐ **The First World War** **A. J. P. Taylor** £3.95

'He manages in some 200 illustrated pages to say almost everything that is important ... A special text ... a remarkable collection of photographs' – *Observer*

A CHOICE OF PENGUINS

☐ *Man and the Natural World* **Keith Thomas** £4.95

Changing attitudes in England, 1500–1800. 'An encyclopedic study of man's relationship to animals and plants . . . a book to read again and again' – Paul Theroux, *Sunday Times* Books of the Year

☐ *Jean Rhys: Letters 1931–66*
Edited by Francis Wyndham and Diana Melly £3.95

'Eloquent and invaluable . . . her life emerges, and with it a portrait of an unexpectedly indomitable figure' – Marina Warner in the *Sunday Times*

☐ *The French Revolution* **Christopher Hibbert** £4.50

'One of the best accounts of the Revolution that I know . . . Mr Hibbert is outstanding' – J. H. Plumb in the *Sunday Telegraph*

☐ *Isak Dinesen* **Judith Thurman** £4.95

The acclaimed life of Karen Blixen, 'beautiful bride, disappointed wife, radiant lover, bereft and widowed woman, writer, sibyl, Scheherazade, child of Lucifer, Baroness; always a unique human being . . . an assiduously researched and finely narrated biography' – *Books & Bookmen*

☐ *The Amateur Naturalist*
Gerald Durrell with Lee Durrell £4.95

'Delight . . . on every page . . . packed with authoritative writing, learning without pomposity . . . it represents a real bargain' – *The Times Educational Supplement*. 'What treats are in store for the average British household' – *Daily Express*

☐ *When the Wind Blows* **Raymond Briggs** £2.95

'A visual parable against nuclear war: all the more chilling for being in the form of a strip cartoon' – *Sunday Times*. 'The most eloquent anti-Bomb statement you are likely to read' – *Daily Mail*

PENGUIN TRAVEL BOOKS

☐ *Arabian Sands* **Wilfred Thesiger**   £3.50

'In the tradition of Burton, Doughty, Lawrence, Philby and Thomas, it is, very likely, the book about Arabia to end all books about Arabia' – *Daily Telegraph*

☐ *The Flight of Ikaros* **Kevin Andrews**   £3.50

'He also is in love with the country . . . but he sees the other side of that dazzling medal or moon . . . If you want some truth about Greece, here it is' – Louis MacNeice in the *Observer*

☐ *D. H. Lawrence and Italy*   £4.95

In *Twilight in Italy, Sea and Sardinia* and *Etruscan Places,* Lawrence recorded his impressions while living, writing and travelling in 'one of the most beautiful countries in the world'.

☐ *Maiden Voyage* **Denton Welch**   £3.50

Opening during his last term at public school, from which the author absconded, *Maiden Voyage* turns into a brilliantly idiosyncratic account of China in the 1930s.

☐ *The Grand Irish Tour* **Peter Somerville-Large**   £4.95

The account of a year's journey round Ireland. 'Marvellous . . . describes to me afresh a landscape I thought I knew' – Edna O'Brien in the *Observer*

☐ *Slow Boats to China* **Gavin Young**   £3.95

On an ancient steamer, a cargo dhow, a Filipino kumpit and twenty more agreeably cranky boats, Gavin Young sailed from Piraeus to Canton in seven crowded and colourful months. 'A pleasure to read' – Paul Theroux

PENGUIN TRAVEL BOOKS

☐ *The Kingdom by the Sea* **Paul Theroux** £2.50

1982, the year of the Falklands War and the Royal Baby, was the ideal time, Theroux found, to travel round the coast of Britain and surprise the British into talking about themselves. 'He describes it all brilliantly and honestly' – Anthony Burgess

☐ *One's Company* **Peter Fleming** £2.95

His journey to China as special correspondent to *The Times* in 1933. 'One reads him for literary delight . . . But, he is also an observer of penetrating intellect' – Vita Sackville West

☐ *The Traveller's Tree* **Patrick Leigh Fermor** £3.95

'A picture of the Indies more penetrating and original than any that has been presented before' – *Observer*

☐ *The Path to Rome* **Hilaire Belloc** £3.95

'The only book I ever wrote for love,' is how Belloc described the wonderful blend of anecdote, humour and reflection that makes up the story of his pilgrimage to Rome.

☐ *The Light Garden of the Angel King* **Peter Levi** £2.95

Afghanistan has been a wild rocky highway for nomads and merchants, Alexander the Great, Buddhist monks, great Moghul conquerors and the armies of the Raj. Here, quite brilliantly, Levi writes about their journeys and his own.

☐ *Among the Russians* **Colin Thubron** £2.95

'The Thubron approach to travelling has an integrity that belongs to another age' – Dervla Murphy in the *Irish Times*. 'A magnificent achievement' – Nikolai Tolstoy

A CHOICE OF
PELICANS AND PEREGRINES

☐ **The Knight, the Lady and the Priest**
  Georges Duby   £5.95

The acclaimed study of the making of modern marriage in medieval France. 'He has traced this story – sometimes amusing, often horrifying, always startling – in a series of brilliant vignettes' – *Observer*

☐ **The Limits of Soviet Power** Jonathan Steele   £3.50

The Kremlin's foreign policy – Brezhnev to Chernenko, is discussed in this informed, informative 'wholly invaluable and extraordinarily timely study' – *Guardian*

☐ **Understanding Organizations** Charles B. Handy   £4.95

Third Edition. Designed as a practical source-book for managers, this Pelican looks at the concepts, key issues and current fashions in tackling organizational problems.

☐ **The Pelican Freud Library: Volume 12**   £4.95

Containing the major essays: *Civilization, Society and Religion, Group Psychology* and *Civilization and Its Discontents*, plus other works.

☐ **Windows on the Mind** Erich Harth   £4.95

Is there a physical explanation for the various phenomena that we call 'mind'? Professor Harth takes in age-old philosophers as well as the latest neuroscientific theories in his masterly study of memory, perception, free will, selfhood, sensation and other richly controversial fields.

☐ **The Pelican History of the World**
  J. M. Roberts   £5.95

'A stupendous achievement . . . This is the unrivalled World History for our day' – A. J. P. Taylor

A CHOICE OF
PELICANS AND PEREGRINES

☐ *A Question of Economics* **Peter Donaldson** £4.95

Twenty key issues – from the City and big business to trades unions – clarified and discussed by Peter Donaldson, author of *10 × Economics* and one of our greatest popularizers of economics.

☐ *Inside the Inner City* **Paul Harrison** £4.50

A report on urban poverty and conflict by the author of *Inside the Third World*. 'A major piece of evidence' – *Sunday Times*. 'A classic: it tells us what it is really like to be poor, and why' – *Time Out*

☐ *What Philosophy Is* **Anthony O'Hear** £3.95

What are human beings? How should people act? How do our thoughts and words relate to reality? Contemporary attitudes to these age-old questions are discussed in this new study, an eloquent and brilliant introduction to philosophy today.

☐ *The Arabs* **Peter Mansfield** £4.95

New Edition. 'Should be studied by anyone who wants to know about the Arab world and how the Arabs have become what they are today' – *Sunday Times*

☐ *Religion and the Rise of Capitalism*
R. H. Tawney £3.95

The classic study of religious thought of social and economic issues from the later middle ages to the early eighteenth century.

☐ *The Mathematical Experience*
Philip J. Davis and Reuben Hersh £6.95

Not since *Gödel, Escher, Bach* has such an entertaining book been written on the relationship of mathematics to the arts and sciences. 'It deserves to be read by everyone ... an instant classic' – *New Scientist*

A CHOICE OF
PELICANS AND PEREGRINES

☐ *Crowds and Power* **Elias Canetti** £4.95

'Marvellous . . . an immensely interesting, often profound reflection about the nature of society, in particular the nature of violence' – Susan Sontag in *The New York Review of Books*

☐ *The Death and Life of Great American Cities*
Jane Jacobs £4.95

One of the most exciting and wittily written attacks on contemporary city planning to have appeared in recent years – thought-provoking reading and, as one critic noted, 'extremely apposite to conditions in the UK'.

☐ *Computer Power and Human Reason*
Joseph Weizenbaum £3.95

Internationally acclaimed by scientists and humanists alike: 'This is the best book I have read on the impact of computers on society, and on technology and on man's image of himself' – *Psychology Today*

These books should be available at all good bookshops or news-agents, but if you live in the UK or the Republic of Ireland and have difficulty in getting to a bookshop, they can be ordered by post. Please indicate the titles required and fill in the form below.

NAME _____ BLOCK CAPITALS

ADDRESS _____

_____

_____

Enclose a cheque or postal order payable to The Penguin Bookshop to cover the total price of books ordered, plus 50p for postage. Readers in the Republic of Ireland should send £1R equivalent to the sterling prices, plus 67p for postage. Send to: The Penguin Bookshop, 54/56 Bridlesmith Gate, Nottingham, NG1 2GP.

You can also order by phoning (0602) 599295, and quoting your Barclaycard or Access number.

Every effort is made to ensure the accuracy of the price and availability of books at the time of going to press, but it is sometimes necessary to increase prices and in these circumstances retail prices may be shown on the covers of books which may differ from the prices shown in this list or elsewhere. This list is not an offer to supply any book.

This order service is only available to residents in the UK and the Republic of Ireland.